TORCH SONG
TRILOGY

TORCH SONG TRILOGY

three plays by
HARVEY FIERSTEIN

with a note from the author

 VILLARD BOOKS / NEW YORK / 1983

Library of Congress Cataloging in Publication Data
Fierstein, Harvey, 1954–
  Torch song trilogy.

  Reprint. Originally published: New York, N.Y. : Gay Presses of New York, 1981.

  Contents: International stud—Fugue in a nursery—Widows and children first!
  I. Title.
PS3556.I4213T6   1983   812′.54   83-48075
ISBN 0-394-53428-X

Manufactured in the United States of America

9 8 7 6 5 4 3 2

First Edition

Photographs Copyright © 1982 by Gerry Goodstein

Book Designed by Oksana Kushnir

For Paul Reese

. . . and with loving memories of Kenn Hill,
Charles Embry, Bud Sherman.
J. Galen McKinley, and my Father.

The author wishes to thank the following people for their help and inspiration: Ray Benkoczy, Helen Hanft, Paul Falzone, Mitchell Maxwell, Helen Merrill, Harvey Tavel, Ronald Tavel, Dorothea Regal, Norman Glick, George Whitmore, Don Shewey, Richard Hale, and a very special thank you to the two people most responsible for bringing this Trilogy to life: Eric Concklin and my "Mama" Ellen Stewart.

AUTHOR'S NOTE

I have been blessed with seven honest, earnest, free-tongued characters who, within these pages, willingly impart more of themselves to you than the closest friends would ever dare. I will therefore leave them to their story-telling with the briefest of Parental Guidance.

Like a gaudy East Indian purse, outrageous in color, embroidered in cliché design, the worth of these plays lies ultimately in the tiny mirrors woven into the fabric wherein we catch our reflections. Perhaps you'll see a little of yourself on the phone with Arnold's "Why don't you love me anymore?" call. Or maybe find yourself in Laurel's "Just because I said that's what I want doesn't mean that I'm ready for it" logic. Or it might be while reading Mrs. Beckoff you'll stop and smile and say, "That's *my* Mother." Any little thing that makes you feel less alone is what and why these plays are.

Not one of the characters you'll meet is "right." There are no answers forthcoming. But you might just catch a line, like an old familiar half-heard song playing on a jukebox, that reaches out and touches something going on inside of you. And for that instant you are relieved of the isolation. That is the worth of a Torch Song. That is the goal of these plays.

TORCH SONG TRILOGY *was first presented on Broadway at the Little Theatre on June 10, 1982, by Kenneth Waissman, Martin Markinson, John Glines, Lawrence Lane, BetMar, and Donald Tick with the following cast:*

ARNOLD	Harvey Fierstein
ED	Court Miller
LADY BLUES	Susan Edwards
LAUREL	Diane Tarleton
ALAN	Paul Joynt
DAVID	Fisher Stevens
MRS. BECKOFF	Estelle Getty

Directed by Peter Pope
Original Score by Ada Janik
Stage Design by Bill Stabile
Musical Direction by Ned Levy
Costumes by Mardi Philips
Lighting by Scott Pinkney
Production Stage Manager: Herb Vogler

TABLE OF CONTENTS

THE TRILOGY

THE INTERNATIONAL STUD

THE INTERNATIONAL STUD *was first presented by La Mama E.T.C. on February 2, 1978, with the following cast:*

LADY BLUES	Diane Tarleton
ARNOLD	Harvey Fierstein
ED	Steve Spiegel

Directed by Eric Concklin
Musical Direction by Ned Levy
Costumes by Mardi Philips
Lighting by Joanna Schielke
Production Stage Manager: B. J. Allen

The production subsequently played at The Player's Theatre with Richard Dow as ED and Lee Evans as Stage Manager.

There is a gay bar in New York City called The International Stud. It boasts a pool table, a pinball machine, and the jump-ingest backroom in town. I dearly dedicate these plays to all who made it their home.

I wish for each of them the courage to leave it when they can, and the good sense to come back when they must.

CHARACTERS

ED REISS: Thirty-four, very handsome; masculine with a boyish charm.

ARNOLD: Twenty-four (going on forty). A kvetch of great wit and want.

LADY BLUES

SYNOPSIS OF SCENES

1) January. Arnold, backstage of a nightclub.
2) February. Ed in The International Stud bar.
3) June. Ed and Arnold in their respective apartments.
4) September. Arnold in The International Stud bar.
5) November. Ed and Arnold backstage.

LADY BLUES

Before Scene 1 and between each of the following scenes, Lady Blues appears on a separate set, atop a grand piano, dressed in period, and sings a 1920s or 1930s torch song in the manner of Helen Morgan or Ruth Etting. The choice of songs I leave to the director, as they should highlight the values of each particular production. They should not comment on the action as much as conjure it. . . .

SIGN LANGUAGE

The signs shown
on this page are used in Scenes 1 and 5.

"Cockroach"—
Wiggle fingers in
shown position.

"I love you"—
Extend thumb,
first finger and
last finger.

"Fuck"—
Knock the two
hands together.

"Not"—
Move hand under and
away from chin.

"Enough"—
Run right hand over cupped left
as if showing the hand were a full cup.

SCENE ONE: ARNOLD

*The play is performed against a black cyclorama with as little actual
scenery as possible. Upstage center a grand piano sits on its platform—
raising Lady Blues high above the action. Downstage of her, on either
side, are three-foot-high platforms which will be the two apartments.
Each has a chair, table, and telephone. Arnold's chair is worn and
comfortable, Ed's is new and straight. Downstage center stands The
International Stud platform. It is just large enough for one person to
stand comfortably and is raised two feet from the stage. Left of it is a
larger platform, six feet by eight feet, which holds an armchair and vanity
table. It is Arnold's dressing room. As the lights come down on Lady
Blues after her opening song, the sounds of a music box are heard softly.
The lights rise on the backstage platform, revealing Arnold in full drag
applying a false eyelash to his face. He turns off the music box. . . . The
lash slips out of place. . . .*

ARNOLD (*To audience*):   Damned Elmer's glue! Just let me finish
emasculating this eye and I'll be right with you. (*Fixes it. Poses in
the mirror.*)

Gorgeous, huh? Use your imagination, it's still under con-
struction.

I think my biggest problem is being young and beautiful.
It is my biggest problem because I have never been young and
beautiful. More importantly, I will never be young and beautiful.
Oh, I've been beautiful. And God knows I've been young. But
never the twain have met. Not so's anyone would notice anyway.
A shrink acquaintance of mine believes this to be the root of my
attraction to a class of men most subtly described as old and ugly.
But I think he's underestimating my wheedles. See, an ugly
person who goes after a pretty person gets nothing but trouble.
But a pretty person who goes after an ugly person gets at least
cabfare.

I ain't sayin' I never fell for a pretty face, but when *"les jeux
sont faits"* . . . give me a toad with a pot of gold and I'll give ya
three meals a day. 'Cause, honeys, ain't no such thing as a toad

when the lights go down. It's either feast or famine. It's the daylight you gotta watch out for. Face it, a thing of beauty is a joy till sunrise.

I never push Lady Luck myself. I got, whatchoo call a extrasensory sense about such things. If I really like a guy, I automatically wake three minutes before him. Giving me just enough time to unsucker my pucker, reinstate my coif, and repose my repose so's his eyes upon waking conjure images by Jove and Lana Turner; guaranteeing my breakfast if not his real phone number.

Here's another hint to all present presently unattached. You can cross any man off your dance card who A: Discusses his wonderful relationship with his mother. B: Discusses his wonderful relationship with his shrinker. Or C: Refuses to discuss his wonderful relationship with his mother or shrinker. See, a guy who's got that kind of confidante is in what I call a "state of confession." And experience has sorely taught me, you can never be more to a man in such a state than subject matter for their conversations. . . .

Not that I got anything against analysis, I don't. I think it's a great way to keep from boring your friends. But what's good for the bored just ain't so for the bed, if you get my drift. See, when there's trouble in Paradise you got two possible M.O.'s. Pull back or push in. But pull back when he's got a professional shoulder to lean on and the entire effect of losing you is shot. Try pushing and you've bought yourself two for one. Push hard enough, and you'll find yourself visiting him Sundays at the "Happy Home for the Bewildered."

Now, I ain't sayin' you should only date sane men (I don't want to kill off all the fish in the polluted sea), but at least find one who's willing to fight on his own. Give me a man with both fists clenched tight . . . and I'll give you a smile from here to next Thursday.

And there's another group you've gotta watch your food stamps around . . . "The Hopeless." They break down into three major categories: Married, "Just in for the Weekend," and terminally ill. Those affairs are the worst. You go into them with

your eyes open, knowing all the limitations and accepting them maturely . . . then wham-bam! . . . You're writing letters to Dear Abby and burning black candles at midnight and you ask yourself, "What happened?" I'll tell you what happened. You got just what you wanted! The person who thinks they's mature enough to handle an affair that's hopeless from the beginning is the very same person who keeps the publishers of Gothic Romances up to their tragic endings in mink; not to mention the reissuers of those twenties torch ditties . . . music to be miserable by.

So, what's left? I don't know. But there are some. I found one once. His name was Charley. He was tall, handsome, rich, deaf. Everything you could want in an affair and more. The deafness was the more. He never screamed at me, all his friends were nice and quiet, I could play music as loud as I liked without ever disturbing his reading, and best of all, I could snore. I even learned me some of that sign language. Wait, I still remember some. Like this here, (*He demonstrates.*) it means cockroach. And this one (*Demonstrates*) means fuck. Here's my favorite. (*Demonstrates*) It means "I love you." And I did. But . . . (*Signing and speaking together*) not enough. I guess I bought them Gothic publishers a few minks of my own.

(*Back to his dressing*) For those of yis what ain't yet guessed I am an entertainer (or what's left of one), I go by the name Virginia Hamm. Ain't that a kick in the rubber parts? You should hear some of my former handles: Kitty Litter, Lorretta Dung, Bertha Venation . . . and I'm plenty tough too. I can afford to be; behind a phony name, face, and figure. But that's all right.

See, I'm among the last of a dying breed. Once the ERA and gay civil rights bills have been passed, me and mine will find ourselves swept under the carpets like the blacks done to Amos, Andy, and Aunt Jemima. But that's all right too. With a voice and face like this I got nothing to worry about, I can always drive a cab. And that, chillun', is called power. Be it gay, black, or flowered, it always comes down to the survival of the majority.

Shit, I'd better get a move on it! (*He takes a roll of toilet paper and unwinds two huge wads.*) Would ya'll mind turning your backs? . . . Well, could you at least close your eyes?

*(He places the paper in his bra with his back to the audience,
turns proudly with his chest held high, catches the unevenness
of the sizes in the mirror, and adjusts them.)*
There are easier things in this life than being a drag queen.
But, I ain't got no choice. Try as I may, I just can't walk in flats.
(Putting on his hat and shoes)
You know what I really want? I want The International
Stud. No, not the bar. The man. A stud. A guy who knows what
he wants and ain't a'scared to go out and get it. A guy who
satisfies his every need, and don't mind if you get what you want
in the bargain. Matter of fact, he aims to please. He'd be happy
to be whatever you wanted him to be, 'cause you're happy bein'
what he wants you to be. The more you put in, the more you
get back. An honest man. The International Stud. One size fits
all. But I wouldn't want no guy that wanted me like this here.
No, I'd need him for the rest of the time. For the other part of
me. The part that's not so well-protected. Oh, there's plenty that
want me like this. And I take their admiration gratefully. But,
at a distance. I guess a drag queen's like bein' an oil painting!
You gotta stand back from it to get the full effect.
(Standing) Well, I think we're in business! My, how time flies
when you's doin' all the talking. *(Tucking in the chair)* Who knows,
maybe my Right Man is out there tonight, right? Y'all take care
now, hear? *(He makes the "I love you" sign, turns to go, stops, and
comes back.)* Ya know . . . in my life I have slept with more men
than are named and/or numbered in the Bible (Old and New
Testaments put together). But in all those beds not once has
someone said, "Arnold, I love you . . ." that I could believe. So,
I ask myself, "Do you really care?" And the only honest answer
I can give myself is, "Yes, I care." I care be— *(Catches himself)* I
care a great deal. But not enough.
*(He smiles knowingly as the lights black out on him and up
on the singer.)*

SCENE TWO: ED

As Lady Blues finishes her song, the sounds of a bar are heard faintly, and the lights reveal Ed standing on The Stud platform, his back to the audience. He is tall, lean, and very handsome. Although he is in his thirties, his greatest charm is his boyishness.

ED (*Suddenly stepping back onto someone's foot*):   Oh, excuse me. I'm sorry. I was just trying to duck that pool cue. Gets pretty crowded in here on a Saturday. Your foot okay? Good.
> (*He turns away, but then can't help sneaking a look at the stranger. He smiles and turns away embarrassed, then turns to him again.*)

No permanent damage, I hope. To your foot I mean. . . . Good.
> (*He turns away again, but still tries to sneak a look behind him. He gathers his courage and confronts the stranger with a huge smile.*)

Look, the name's Ed Reiss. My friends call me Ed. (*No response*) I'm Sagittarius. . . . What's so funny? . . . Oh, well, some people like to know that stuff. I don't believe in any of it myself, but I have done some reading about it. See, I like to know what's expected of me. (*He stares with a huge grin.*) You have a beautiful smile. . . . No, really, you do. Can I get you another beer?

All right, one Lite coming up. (*To bartender*) Can I have a Lite, please?

No, not a match. I meant a Lite beer. (*To stranger*) Am I speaking English? I feel like I'm a Martian or something. I think it's that smile of yours. Say, what's your name?

Arnold? Your friends call you Arnie or Arn?

Arnold. Well, nice to meet you, Arnold. (*Handing money to the*

bartender) Here you go. (*Beer to Arnold*) And here you go. Are you Italian?

Spanish?

Jewish?! I never would have guessed it. Not with those dark romantic eyes. I don't remember ever seeing you here before. I don't get in that often myself. I teach over in Brooklyn and so have to be up and out pretty early, so if I'm feeling horny, this is where I come. I can be in and out of the backroom and home in bed within an hour.

No. I'm off tomorrow. That's why I'm out here instead of back there. You really do have beautiful eyes. Are you wearing makeup?

I didn't think so. So . . . uh . . . how's the backroom? Crowded, I'll bet.

Never?

No, it's just that you don't expect to meet someone in a backroom bar who's never been in the backroom. Are you here with a friend?

Is he your lover?

So, you're unattached. How lucky for me. Where you from?

Sure, I know where that is. Live alone?

Well, look, I have a car . . . I'd ask you back to my place, but I have this straight roommate. He's got a hang-up about gays. It's really his place. I only sublet from him.

Oh, well, I date women too. So . . . Anyway, I really live upstate. I've got a farm up about an hour from Montreal. That's my real home. I spend the weekends there during the school year and then all of my summer vacation. I own half of Walton Mountain.

No, that's really what it's called. Most of the land is trees, but there's a piece of flat farming land with an old barn and I work a half acre of that. I grow all my own vegetables. I've even got a small vineyard. The mountains have some great white water for canoeing, and in the winter . . . it's a skier's dream. You ski?

Would you like to learn?

All right, it's a deal. You'll love the house, it's really great. One of those old Victorian farmhouses with lots of gingerbread and Franklin stoves. My father and I are restoring it.

Well, my parents winter in Florida but come North to stay with me in the warmer months. Hey, wha'd'ya say we continue this conversation in the car?

Great. By the way, what do you do?

No, I meant for a living.

Can you really make a living doing that?

I do believe you're the first one I've met . . . personally. Ready? (*Putting on his coat*) The car's just across the street. Anyone ever tell you you have a very sexy voice? You really do. Is it natural or do you have a cold? (*Gesturing*) After you.

> (*He turns as the lights go out on the platform and come up on the singer.*)

RADIO SHOW BETWEEN

The following conversation should be tape-recorded and played during Lady Blues's third song. She should listen to it as if it were part of the musical break. It is underscored by the piano.

ED (*Excited*):   Oh, wow. Your place is really great.

ARNOLD: I'm glad you like it.

ED: No, it's really fabulous. But, would you mind putting on a light?

ARNOLD: There's not much to see.

ED: There's you.

ARNOLD (*Embarrassed giggle, sound of light switch*):   Better?

ED: Better . . . and better. You're shaking.

ARNOLD: Nervous, I guess.

ED: Me, too.

ARNOLD: Really?

ED: Really.

ARNOLD: I'm glad you asked me home.

ED: Me too.

ARNOLD: Ed?

ED: Yeah?

ARNOLD: I feel . . . I don't know . . . kinda scared.

ED: Better?

ARNOLD: Better . . . and better.
    (*They both laugh intimately as Lady Blues continues her song.*)

SCENE THREE

The lights come up on Arnold in his apartment. He sits on the floor in shorts and a sweat shirt with a paperback stuck in his mouth. It is The I Ching. *He is throwing coins and marking the hexagram nervously. Reading . . .*

ARNOLD: "Having completed the hexagram, compare it to the chart on page 228." (*He flips to the chart and compares his scratchings to it.*) Here it is. Number thirty-eight. (*He searches excitedly for the right page. He finds it.*) Here we go. "Hexagram Thirty-eight, Koo-eee-iiiii. The Estranged."

(*He is struck by its meaning and hides the book under the chair. He lights a cigarette while staring at the phone. He climbs into the chair, grabs the phone into his lap, and dials.*) Hello, Murray? Call me back.

(*He slams down the receiver and freezes, his hand perched over the phone ready to lift it as soon as it rings. It does not. Slowly his face begins to crack with worry. Still the phone does not ring. He is practically in frozen hysteria when suddenly it does ring.*)

ARNOLD (*Grabbing it angrily*): Goddammit, Murray, what took you so long? . . . The shower could have waited, Murray. . . . The shampoo in the shower could have waited, Murray. . . . The man with the shampoo in the shower could have waited, Murray. Anyway, I can't talk now. I gotta keep the line free. (*Starting to hang up*) What? . . . I just wanted to make sure the phone was working. . . . Ed. All right? I'm expecting a call from Ed. . . . When? Well, it is now Tuesday, eight P.M. Well, Ed's gonna call sometime after Tuesday eight P.M. . . . Of course he's gonna call, Murray. You think I'd sit by the phone for six days if he wasn't gonna call? . . . You are getting on my nerves, Murray. Look, he is a very busy man. With a great many responsibilities. He will call me when he is able. And I will understand. Got it? When you have been seeing someone

for four months, Murray, you build a relationship based on trust and mutual respect. Something you and your Magic Fingers shower massage would not understand. He will call, Murray. He knows when he's got a good thing going. He knows I ain't like those other cheap tricks he sees. He knows I got something that puts me above those runned-up-the-mill, always-on-Sunday, anyplace-I-hang-my-crotch-is-home variety of homosexual commonly cruised in these here parts. I am important, Murray. But most of all, Murray, I am mysterious. Which is a quality you don't find on every bar stool. (*Getting slow and sexy*) Oh, no, Murray, he will call. And when he does . . . and when he does . . . and when he does . . . (*Jumping suddenly*) the phone's gonna be free! (*Slams down the phone*) (*Pouting*) O ye of little faith!

> (*Arnold gets an idea. He puts out his cigarette, takes the phone in hand, takes two real deep breaths, and holds them and dials. The phone in Ed's apartment rings as the lights come up, revealing Ed dressed neatly for a date, just about to open a bottle of red wine. There are two glasses on the table by the phone.*)

ED (*Lifting the receiver*):   Hello?

ARNOLD (*Letting out his breath in pants*):   Hi. Was that you?

ED (*Recognizing the voice. Slightly uneasy.*):   Oh, hi. Was what me?

ARNOLD: Just now on the phone. Was that you trying to get me?

ED: No.

ARNOLD: Oh. Then I wonder who it was. See, I just walked in this second. (*Nonstop*) You know, I've been out of town all week. And I was fumbling at the door with my luggage and the keys when I heard the phone ringing, so of course I dropped the keys, and when I bent over to pick up the keys I dropped the luggage, so of course since I was nervous and the phone was ringing one of the cases uncaught and opened up and everything fell out all over the place. So, finally I got the door open and kicked everything inside, dove at the phone,

and picked it up just in time to hear whoever it was calling hang up. (*Slight nervous laugh, then quietly, almost sadly*) So, how are you?

ED (*Gently*):   I was going to call you real soon. I've just been really busy.

ARNOLD: What's the difference, we're talking now. By the way, you remember that Helen Morgan record I played last time you were here? Well, I was able to find another copy in a little secondhand shop uptown. It's almost like new. So I picked it up for you.

ED (*Embarrassed*):   Thanks.

ARNOLD: You're welcome.

ED: Look, Arnold, I can't talk right now. I've got a friend coming over for dinner and uh . . .

ARNOLD: That's okay. I just called 'cause I thought it was you calling. So, give me a call when you're not so busy.

ED (*Guilty*):   I'm sorry. I'll call you tomorrow.

ARNOLD (*Hurting*):   Hey, no problem. I understand.

ED (*Annoyed suddenly*):   What do you understand? You never give me a chance to call you. Every time I'm just about to, there you are calling me.

ARNOLD (*Frightened*):   ESP maybe? (*No response*) Well, just think of all the money I save you on phone calls.

ED (*Gently amused*):   You're impossible. You know that?

ARNOLD (*Relaxing a bit*):   Yeah. It's a wonder you put up with me.

ED (*Checks his watch*):   So, how was your trip?

ARNOLD: My trip? Oh, my trip. Okay. Who's coming over for dinner.

ED: A friend. You don't know him.

ARNOLD: How do you know? I know lots of hymns: "Battle Hymn of the Republic," "Rock of Ages," "O Come, Emmanuel". . . .

ED: You are impossible.

ARNOLD: So, is it an old him or a new him?

ED (*Tightening*):   Why do you do this to yourself?

ARNOLD: I'm just asking. Can't a person show a little interest in another person's life? (*Pause*) So?

ED: A new one.

ARNOLD (*Definitely wounded but smiling through*):   Aha. Where'd you meet him? The Stud?

ED: I've really got to go now, Arnold. I'll call you soon, all right?

ARNOLD: That's what you said last week.

ED: Well, maybe if you waited and gave me a chance to call . . .

ARNOLD (*Letting go*):   That's all I'm asking *you* for: a chance. Why're you treating me like some trick you picked up last night?

ED (*Angry*):   Arnold, I don't want a scene on the phone. I'll call you tomorrow and we'll get together and talk.

ARNOLD (*Real soft*):   What's wrong? Until last week, I could've sworn things were going great for both of us. What's happening?

ED: Not now, Arnold.

ARNOLD: Yes. Now.

ED: Arnold, I'm just going to get angry.

ARNOLD: So get angry! Just talk to me! (*Silence*) Hello? Are you there?

ED (*Pause. Quietly.*):   I'm here.

ARNOLD (*Soft*):   I miss you. (*Pause*) I think about you all the time. (*Pause*) I'm so damned horny.

ED (*Slight laugh*): You need a job.

ARNOLD: I've got a job. I need a lover.

ED (*Hard*): Well, I don't. There. Is that what you wanted to hear?

ARNOLD: No. But it's a beginning. What *do* you need?

ED: A friend. I've said that all along. If you'd listen sometimes instead of . . .

ARNOLD: You've got a friend. And a lover too. All in one neat package. That's modern efficiency at work.

ED: It is not what I need.

ARNOLD: How do you know? Maybe it is. You'll never be sure unless you give it a try.

ED: I have tried, Arnold.

ARNOLD (*Hard*): No you haven't! (*Softer*) You haven't. I wish to God you had, but you haven't.

ED: Arnold, this is not going to do any good for either one of us.

ARNOLD: What makes you so sure of what's good and what's not? Maybe it's just what we need. Maybe it's just what *I* need. You can't expect me to just sit around here waiting for you to call.

ED: I never asked you to. I told you to go out, have a good time, meet other people . . .

ARNOLD: I can't, all right? I'm not built that way.

ED: Well, I'm just not ready to make that kind of a commitment.

ARNOLD: I'm not asking you to. But if I have to accept you going out, then you have to accept that I'm not.

ED (*Puzzled*): You really are crazy.

ARNOLD: I'm lonely.

ED: That's not my fault.

ARNOLD: Wanna bet?

ED: You've got no right to make me feel guilty.

ARNOLD: I happen to be in love with you. That must give me some kind of rights. And if that don't give me the right to see you, then at least I got the right to bitch about it. (*Long silence*) You said that you loved me. You do remember telling me that, don't you?

ED (*Quietly*):   Yes.

ARNOLD: Then, do you or don't you?

ED: You know how I feel about you.

ARNOLD: I don't. I wouldn't ask if I did.

ED: Yes. I love you.

ARNOLD: Then what's going on?

ED: What do you want me to say?

ARNOLD: I want you to say what's on your mind. That's what I want. I want you to tell me how in two short weeks we have gone from being lovers to whatever the hell you'd call this?

ED (*Trying to retain cool*):   You are being very difficult.

ARNOLD (*Mimicking*):   You are being very difficult. (*Hard*) Talk to me, goddammit! (*Silence*) Is it your parents coming North? Is that it? Are you ashamed of me?

ED: Of course not.

ARNOLD: Then what?

ED: Not on the phone. What if I come over straight from school tomorrow?

ARNOLD: No! I've got to hear it now. I know what'll happen if you come over, everything will be great just like it always is

when we're together and we'll never even mention tonight. No, I want to hear it from this side of you.

ED (*Checking his watch nervously*):   Arnold, I really cannot talk to you now. She'll be here any minute. I'll see you after work tomorrow, okay? (*No response*) Arnold? Hello?

ARNOLD (*Disbelief*):   She? Did you say SHE?

ED (*Mumbled*):   Shit.

ARNOLD: Oh, "Shit"! Thank God. For a minute I thought you said "She."

ED: I did say she. I am seeing a woman.

ARNOLD: And you called *me* crazy!

ED: Now you know why I didn't want to discuss it on the phone.

ARNOLD: Oh, sure. I can see how much more understandable it would be discussed calmly over a postsexual cigarette. (*Long pause*) It *is* your parents.

ED: No, it isn't!

ARNOLD: Then why all of a sudden like this?

ED: It's not all of a sudden. I just happened to meet her now, that's all. Don't make believe I never told you about my relationships with women.

ARNOLD: Sure, you told me about your woman relations. But I thought you meant sisters and aunts and nieces.

ED: That's not funny.

ARNOLD: I think it's hysterical. (*Long pause. He tries to remain calm.*) So . . . how long has this been going on?

ED: Not long.

ARNOLD: How'd you meet her?

ED: My friends Bob and Janet asked me if I was seeing anyone because they knew this girl they thought I might like to meet.

ARNOLD: And what did you say when they asked if you were seeing anyone?

ED: I said that I wasn't. (*Guilty pause*) Well, I could hardly tell them about you, could I?

ARNOLD: God forbid!

ED (*Silence. Quietly.*):   What are you thinking?

ARNOLD: I am thinking about how it feels to be a no one in the life of someone you love. (*Pause*) Tell me about her.

ED (*Uneasy*):   Why don't you call me a bastard and hang up?

ARNOLD: I want to understand. Talk to me.

ED: I can't . . .

ARNOLD: Please.

ED: Well, she's wonderful.

ARNOLD: Bastard!

ED: You asked!

ARNOLD: I did, didn't I. It's the masochist in me. What'd you tell her about me?

ED: Nothing.

ARNOLD: That does seem to be my name. You did tell her you were bisexual, didn't you?

ED: No. I didn't think it was important.

ARNOLD: Of course not. How silly of me to even mention it.

ED: I'm not so sure that some secrets aren't better kept that way.

ARNOLD: You don't feel that's just slightly dishonest?

ED: No. We have a more mature relationship than that.

ARNOLD: Pardon my naiveté. I didn't know that there really was

such a thing as "love with the proper stranger." So, when are you taking her to meet your parents?

ED: This weekend.

ARNOLD: I don't believe a word of this. And you're still going to tell me that they have nothing to do with this sudden burst of heterosexuality? (*No response*) Look, Ed, I don't know much about the straight world, but I do know that when a guy takes a gal to meet his folks, for the weekend no less, that this is no casual affair. (*No response*) Don't you feel you're being unfair to lead her on that way? (Not to mention what you're doing to me.) (*No response*) Don't you think she has a right to know what she's letting herself in for? (*No response*) What's the matter? Catch your tongue in the closet door?

ED: You're really dragging me over the coals.

ARNOLD: Why should I be the only one with a barbecued ass? If I may ask another stupid question: What am I supposed to do?

ED: That's up to you.

ARNOLD: Not entirely.

ED: I had hoped that we could go on seeing each other. You may not believe this, but I really don't want to lose you.

ARNOLD: That's hitting below the belt; appealing to my Susan Hayward fantasies. . . . "Arnold, Back Street Woman"!

ED: That's not the way it is at all!

ARNOLD: Then take me to meet your parents.

ED: I could if I wanted to. They'd understand.

ARNOLD: Oh, I know they'd understand. It's you that can't. At least you didn't lie when you said you weren't scared for them to meet me. You're scared they'll meet you!

ED: Thank you very much. Your kindness is appreciated.

ARNOLD: Listen, Mr. Reiss. At this moment I don't think you

have a right to expect me to be kind. (*Pulling back*) I'm sorry, I just feel so helpless.

ED (*Slight relaxing laugh*):   You helpless?

ARNOLD (*Laughing too*):   Dumb, huh? (*Cracking*) I don't understand. I thought . . . we were so happy. That we were so special. The way we made love . . . the way you cried in my arms. . . . You said you loved me. . . .

ED: I do. I always will.

ARNOLD (*Desperately*):   Then what are we doing?

ED: I don't know. I'm confused . . . I'm frightened.

ARNOLD: Ed, come over.

ED: No, I can't. I have made up my mind. I know what I want. I'm doing what I have to do. I know that you are hurting, but that is my decision.

ARNOLD: You can't see what you're doing.

ED: Yes I can. I'm not like you, Arnold. I can't be happy living in a ghetto of gay bars and gay restaurants and backrooms, scared that someone will find out that I'm gay and maybe get me fired. I hate those queens with their bitchy remarks and Bette Davis imitations. I don't want any part of that.

ARNOLD: But that's not us. . . .

ED: I want more. I've got to be proud of who I am.

ARNOLD: How can sleeping with a woman make you proud of yourself if you know you'd rather be with a man? How can you ever get any respect from anyone if you won't be yourself? There's no you to respect!

ED: And just where's your self-respect? Huh? I certainly don't see any here!

ARNOLD: You wanna see my self-respect? Here's my self-respect! (*He slams down the receiver as the light blacks out on Ed. Then . . . calmer.*) I fell right into that one.
    (*The lights fade out on Arnold as the singer is once again brought into focus.*)

SCENE FOUR: ARNOLD

The bar sounds are heard again as the lights reveal Arnold standing on The Stud platform dressed in denims and swigging from a beer can.

ARNOLD: Look, Murray, I am not that lonely! This here's as far as I go. My standards may lie just left of reactionary, but my limit in a backroom bar is the front room. Maybe I just better go home, huh? Thank you for taking me out but . . .

It just ain't my kind of thing, ya know? I realize you may find this hard to comprehend, you bein' the way you are, but, Murray, I am just not that way inclined. I mean, I'm that way inclined, but I'm not that way inclined. Ya know what I mean, Murray? I mean, maybe I'm old-fashioned but I like my sex in a bed. I don't see sex as a spectator sport. I like that one sneaked kiss in the elevator on the way to a man's apartment. I like the apologies he makes for the mess the place is in. I dig the dainty tour and arty conversation while he's dimming the lights and pouring the drinks. I like never finishing those drinks. See, Murray, to me a lap in the bed is worth three in a bar. 'Cause deep down in my heart I know they do not marry sluts. No, they don't, Murray. And it hurts me, Murray, it truly does, to see this multitude of men so love-starved that they resort to sex in a dirty backroom instead of the way God meant us to be. It is cheap, Murray. And I refuse on moral grounds to support the degradation these men have brought themselves to. Period.

Why is it so important to you that I go into that backroom? Are you a'scared to go in there by yourself? Is that it, Murray? Have I hit on the nail? C'mon, level it, Murray, are you a'scared?

I am not a'scared, Murray. Oh no I'm not.

All right, I'll prove it to you. We'll go back there together. But I'm tellin' you now, I ain't doin' nothin'. Okay?

Okay. Let's go. (*He starts to turn tentatively and suddenly spins back.*) Murray, quick, hold my hand. I'm a'scared! What if nobody back there wants me? It's one thing to go into a regular bar and not get picked up. I mean that happens all the time to lots of people for lots of reasons but, Murray, to go into a place like that and get rejected . . . I don't think I could take it. I know I got personal qualities that put me above and beyond the norm: quick mind, sharp wit, glowing personality. But, Murray, what if I don't glow in the dark?

No, I'm okay. Really. Look, it'll take more than a backroom to set me back. After all, I am an Advocate Experience graduate. Poise, confidence, an open mind . . . they'll never put me away! Lead on.

(*He turns his back to the audience as the lights change to dark red. When he faces front again he is groping to find his way. Loud whisper.*)
Murray? Where are you? Murray? Murray? Oh, there you are. Well, it certainly is dark back here. Hang on a second.
(*He takes out a book of matches and lights one. He looks around slowly with gaping mouth.*) Oh, my God! (*He blows out the match.*) Murray, quick, let's get outta here. This ain't no place for someone who goes to confessional. I'd jam up the booth for months! (*He freezes. Whispers.*) Murray, Murray? Someone's got his hand on my crotch. What should I do? (*He tries to smile and look natural, then he grabs the hand and shakes it.*) Hi there. My name is Arnold, what's yours? Where'd he go, Murray? Oh, Murray, I gotta get outta here. I should've never come.

No, I didn't come, Murray! Let's just go, huh? Uh-oh. Murray? Someone's got his hand on my heiney. Can you see what he looks like?

Yes, it does make a difference, Murray! Murray? Murray? He's reaching around front and opening my belt. Murray? Murray? He's opening my zipper. Murray? Murray? . . . What do I do . . . with the beer can?

(*He bends over to put the beer can on the ground when he is suddenly penetrated.*)

MURRAYYYYYYY!!!!!!!

(*At first Arnold's face is twisted in pain and embarrassment as he sways with the humping rhythm. He tries to smile and look comfortable. He feels out the rhythm and quietly enjoys himself for a moment, then he looks unattached, almost bored.*) (*Conversationally*) You come here often? (*The stud hits him on the shoulder.*) No, I don't have to talk. No, that's perfectly all right. I mean, it's not part of my fantasy or anything, conversation, that is. Though I must admit I am prone to sweet nothings deftly whispered. However, they are not essential to my enjoyment of the lovemaking experience. I much prefer to open my senses completely to the moment thereby retaining more of an impression whereon to draw on later dates. If you get my drift.

You do? (*He gets hit again.*) But you'd rather I shut up anyway. Okay. I'm not offended. I realize that it must take a lot of concentration for you to keep your . . . concentration in a situation like this so I won't say another word. Okay? Okay. (*Long pause. He looks around. Adjusts his hands. Then fumbles for a cigarette.*) Cigarette? Oh, I'll save you one for later. Mind if I . . . that's very understanding of you.

(*He lights a match and tries to light the cigarette but can't because of the motion. He grabs the stud's rear and stops him, lights up, then taps him to begin again. Arnold positions his hands in a casual smoker's pose and looks about, puffing deeply.*) Got a nice crowd tonight. Ya know, this here's easier than I thought it would be. See, I don't usually do this sort of thing, but what with breaking from my lover and all . . . But it's not as bad as I thought it would be. I guess that has a lot to do with you. Your attitude, I mean. I find that being a sensitive person, as I am, that I pick up easily on people's vibrations and hence incorporate them into myself. See, I figured I'd be too uptight to allow for such things. But since you obviously don't care, then I don't care. Just another bar, right? Just another night out? Very practical idea. I mean, say you'd picked me up in another bar, well, it might've taken an hour for us to

get to this. Or maybe we wouldn't've gotten along and so never got to find out that we really were so compatible. But this way we can build a relationship the other way around, right? You know, I really like you. Maybe that's a stupid thing to say in a place like this. But if you think about it, it's not so stupid at a time like this, is it? I can't wait to see what you look like.

(*Hit again*) Oh, I'm sorry. I was talking again, wasn't I? Gee, I'm really sorry. It must be my nerves. I guess I'm not as relaxed as I thought 'cause when I get nervous I just talk insistently. On any subject, it don't matter. You just name a subject when I'm nervous and I will talk on and on about it. It don't matter what: sex, drugs, religion, rummage sales, anything. Try it. You'll see. Name a subject. (*The stud pulls out suddenly.*) Oh, you're finished? That was quick. Must'a been hot to trot, huh? (*Miming pulling back on his clothes*) I'd like you to meet this friend of mine. His name is Murray. He must be right around here somewhere. Murray? Murray? Oh, there you are. Murray, I'd like you to meet . . . Hey, I never did catch your naa . . . (*He split.*) Yoo-hoo! Hello? Where'd he go? See, Murray, that's what I've got against places like this. You meet someone nice and you lose him in the dark. I know, I'll light a match. Oh, I don't know what he looks like. Of course, how dumb of me, he's gone out front to wait for me 'cause of the crowd and the smell. C'mon, Murray. Let's go find him.

Wha'd'ya mean, he won't be there? I'm sure he really liked me. He made love to me, didn't he? Well, didn't he? (*Long pause*) Let's get outta here.

(*Arnold turns his back as the normal bar lights return. He squints and tries to smile.*) Well, at least I don't have to cook him breakfast. (*Slow fade. Black.*)

(*Lady Blues sings her final song.*)

SCENE FIVE

The lights come up on the dressing room set again. Ed enters tentatively, looks around, checks his watch, and then sits on the chair at the vanity. He looks at the cards and notes scattered around the mirror and table. He looks uncomfortable. He checks out the makeup on the table and picks up a powder puff as Arnold enters. He stops short in the doorway and stares at Ed, who has not heard him come in. There is a great sadness in Arnold's face. He puts on a huge smile and enters. Arnold is in a dressing robe.

ARNOLD: Careful, some of that might rub off on you.

ED (*Jumping up*): You scared me. (*Holding out his arms*) Hello, Arnold.

ARNOLD (*Walking right past him*): Hello.

ED: Bet you thought you'd never see me again. (*Pause*) You look fantastic.

ARNOLD (*In grand Bette Davis*): Well, aren't you a deah to say so!

ED: The stage manager said it'd be all right for me to wait for you in your dressing room. You don't mind, do you? (*No response. Arnold sits and begins to peel his face off.*) When I asked for you as Arnold he didn't know who I meant. (*A little laugh*) You look beautiful . . . really. Lost a little weight, I see. (*He reaches out to touch Arnold.*)

ARNOLD (*Stiffening*): Please . . .

ED (Pulling back): Sorry. I guess you're still pretty angry, huh?

ARNOLD: No, I'm not *still* angry. This is brand-new. What are you doing here?

ED: I wanted to see you. I've been worried about you. (*Arnold shoots him a look.*) I wanted to make sure that you were all right.

ARNOLD: How'd you know I was here?

ED: I saw an ad in the paper.

ARNOLD: That ad should have satisfied your curiosity.

ED: I had planned on seeing the show and just leaving, but when I saw you onstage I had to come back and talk to you. (*Pause*) Been a long time.

ARNOLD: Five months ago you checked out on me with a single phone call. You said that you knew what you wanted and that I wasn't it. I haven't heard a word from you since. What do you want?

ED: Just to see you.

ARNOLD: You've seen me. Get out.

ED: Arnold, please. I'd like to talk to you.

ARNOLD: No.

ED: Wait, just listen to me for a minute.

ARNOLD: NO!

ED: It's got nothing to do with us . . .

ARNOLD: I said no, goddammit! Now, just go and leave me alone. (*Softer*) The one nice thing I could say about you was when you left, you left. No matter what I thought of your reasons or lack of them, you kept your word. . . .

ED: You knew I'd come back to see you. I told you that I wanted us to be friends. You mean a lot to me. (*Pause. He makes the "I love you" sign and holds it up.*) Arnold? . . .

ARNOLD: Don't get cute with me.

ED: Maybe I shouldn't have come here, but as long as the harm's done can't I talk to you? Just until you're dressed? It's important to me.

ARNOLD (*Indicating a folding chair against the wall*):   Sit down.

ED (*He gets the chair and sets it behind Arnold.*):   So, how you been?

ARNOLD: Can we somehow manage to skip the little niceties and get right to the meat. I know you're here for something.

ED: There is something I have to tell you, but give me a little time. It's not the kind of thing I can blurt right out.

ARNOLD (*Resigned*):   How are your folks?

ED: They're fine. My father had a little trouble with an inner ear infection, but it cleared up nicely.

ARNOLD: They go back South for the winter?

ED: They left two days ago.

ARNOLD: Two days?! What took you so long?

ED: What?

ARNOLD: Ed, you can forget it. It's over. You are not coming back.

ED: You don't understand . . .

ARNOLD: I have never done time in the closet and I sure as hell ain't gettin' in one for you.

ED: But, I don't want to come back. (*Arnold stares.*) Really. Things are going great with Laurel. I tried to tell you. I came to talk to you as a friend. (*Arnold turns back to the mirror. Ed continues merrily.*) We spent a really fantastic summer upstate. We stayed at my parents' place in Florida for a week, then back up to the farm. I got a lot done on the house, including a new chimney.

ARNOLD: And what'd you do with what's-her-face?

ED: Laurel. Well, at first things were sort of strained. She'd hang around me all the time wanting us to work together. But I talked to her and finally she began doing things on her own. It was hard for her to understand. She doesn't take criticism very well. She tenses up and gets very quiet. Mid-August my sister sent her two kids up for a few days and Laurel took care

of them. It was really a marvelous experience for both of us. Sort of like having a family of our own.

ARNOLD: Sounds wonderful! Pa out in the fields, Ma tendin' the young'uns, Grandma and Grandpa rockin' on the porch. I'm just sorry you and Laurel couldn't have spent the summer together.

ED (*Missing that*):   You should have seen how Laurel cried when the kids left. But that was nothing compared to the way she carried on when we came back to the city.

ARNOLD: Sounds like she does a lot of crying.

ED: Not so much anymore. We had a talk about that.

ARNOLD: Sounds like you do a lot of talking.

ED: We have a very honest relationship.

ARNOLD: I can see that. You two living together now?

ED: No. We haven't made that kind of commitment yet. To tell you the truth I'm not sure I could take being with her all the time. She has a way of closing in on me. Actually, it was much easier spending time with you. More relaxed. You're easier to talk to. (*Pause*) I thought about you a lot up there. We would have had a great time.

ARNOLD: I'm not the farmgirl type.

ED: No, you would have loved it. (*Pause*) I worried about you; how you were getting along.

ARNOLD: You could have called and found out.

ED: I thought about it. Once, when everyone was out of the house, I even started dialing.

ARNOLD: What happened?

ED: I didn't think it was fair to build up your hopes.

ARNOLD (*Dreamily*):   There's just one thing I regret about our affair.

ED (*Sincerely*):   What's that?

ARNOLD: That I never beat the shit out of you!

ED: You *are* still angry.

ARNOLD: Where's a tape recorder? No one would ever believe this.

ED: Maybe I'd better go.

ARNOLD: No, please, I'm sorry. Stay, we'll have some wine.

ED: What kind?

ARNOLD (*Producing a gallon and cups*):   House white. Buck-fifty a gallon! You do the honors.

ED (*Pouring*):   Kinda warm, isn't it?

ARNOLD (*Taking his cup*):   But cooling off nicely. I'm glad you came.

ED: So am I. (*Takes a sip and gags*) God! How do you drink this stuff?

ARNOLD (*Taking his cup away from him and pouring the wine into his own*):   In large doses. So, tell me, how's your sex life?

ED (*Caught off guard for a moment*):   . . . Great.

ARNOLD (*Sure of himself*):   As good as with me?

ED: You're doing it again! Asking questions that you really don't want the answers to.

ARNOLD: Maybe I do.

ED: Arnold, I'm not sure the sex we had was always as good for me as it was for you. Sometimes I felt it got out of control.

ARNOLD: Meaning what?

ED: I don't know. Those last few times, it was like losing myself. I remember once, I don't even think I was conscious. All I remember was kissing you and then nothing until waking in your arms, my body all wet. . . .

ARNOLD: And that's bad?

ED: It's not what I want.

ARNOLD: Funny; it's what I pray for.

ED: Well, that's fine when you're twenty-four. But I'm going on thirty-four. I have other needs.

ARNOLD (*Quietly*):   Look at us together in the mirror. Now, who would ever believe that you were ten years older than me? I'm aging about as well as a Beach Party movie.

ED: You're beautiful.

ARNOLD: Is *that* why you left?

ED: I didn't leave you because Laurel was prettier.

ARNOLD: I know that. I've seen her. (*Pause*) That morning, after the phone call, I waited in a cab across from your building and watched the two of you leave for work. I was pretty shocked.

ED: We can't all look like Virginia Hamm. I happen to think she's very beautiful.

ARNOLD: Where would you be now if I was a woman?

ED: What?

ARNOLD: If I was a woman. Who would you be with?

ED: But you're not.

ARNOLD: But if I was. Would you ever even have looked at her?

ED: I love her, Arnold.

ARNOLD: Like you loved me?

ED: Like I could never love you.

ARNOLD: Because you never did love me. You were too busy running scared to love me. You were scared I'd leave you. Scared . . . someone would find out about us. Scared . . . you'd let yourself free for once in your life. Oh, I'm vain enough

to think you could have loved me, but I don't think you had the time.

ED (*Quietly*):   I did love you. Everything would be very easy for me if I didn't. But I do. (*Long silence*) Sometimes . . . sometimes when I have trouble reaching orgasm I imagine you behind me just about to . . .

ARNOLD: Does she know? (*Ed shakes his head.*) Have you talked about me at all?

ED: She knows your name. She found one of the drawings you made. The one of the tree outside my dining-room window. She may know more. I saw her looking at that music book you gave me. She didn't say anything, but remember you wrote poems to me on half the pages. (*Long pause*) I couldn't, Arnold. It's not what I want.

ARNOLD: What did you want to tell me. Huh? (*Softly*) You can talk to me. I'll understand.

ED: It's nothing really. Just a dream I had last week. I dreamt that I was in my parents' house and I went down to my father's workshop and got an old rag and a can of turpentine. Then I went to the kitchen and got a plastic bag. I took all the stuff back up to my bedroom, where I soaked the rag in the turpentine and put it into the plastic bag. Then I got into bed, made myself comfortable, pulled the covers right up to my neck, and then put the plastic bag over my head. The strangest part was as I gathered all the stuff, as I got into bed, as I began blacking out from the fumes . . . I was enjoying myself, laughing up a storm. (*Break*) The phone woke me in the morning. It was Laurel. I couldn't understand what she was saying. Half of me was trying to listen to her, the other half trying to figure out the dream. I felt dizzy as I went back to bed, and there, on the pillow, was the plastic bag with the turpentine-soaked rag. (*Long pause*) I couldn't tell anyone else about it. (*Taking Arnold's hand*) This is what I've always wanted: you and me together talking. I think I love you more now than ever.
    (*Arnold's eyes widen, he jumps up suddenly and begins*

*punching Ed wildly. Ed grabs hold of Arnold's arms and
stretches them out to either side, so that they stand face-to-
face. They freeze for a moment searching each other's eyes,
then suddenly they are in each other's arms, crying, holding
each other tightly.)*

ED: I'm so scared. I need you.

ARNOLD *(Gently releasing himself)*:   Okay. Time out. Everybody
back to his corner.
*(Ed sits back down as Arnold crosses to the vanity. Arnold
is in turmoil. Finally in mock of his opening speech.)*
Wha' happened?!!
*(He laughs instead of crying. Crosses behind Ed and ten-
tatively puts his hands on Ed's shoulders. Ed quickly takes
them into his. Indecision . . .)*
You feel better?

ED *(Happy to be home)*:   Yes.

ARNOLD: Good. Then get out! *(He grabs back his hands angrily.)*
Do you have any idea of what the last five months have been
like for me? I cried on so many shoulders . . . I'm sure I lost
half my friends. But I always knew you'd be back. But I thought
that when you did come back . . . I don't know, that you'd
finally have your shit together. And here you are, more fucked
up than ever. *(Still indecision)* Have you got your car with you?
(Ed nods) Go get it. I'll . . . I'll get dressed and meet you out
front.

ED: Want me to drive you home?

ARNOLD: Huh?

ED *(Rising)*:   I'll get the car. *(He exits.)*
*(Arnold watches him leave, then suddenly snaps himself to
work. He sits at the vanity and quickly brushes out his hair,
clears the tabletop and begins to undress when just as suddenly he stops and stares at the audience, searching each
face.)*

ARNOLD *(Slowly . . . innocently)*:   So, what now? Huh? If I take

him back now, knowing all I do, maybe I could make it work. With a little understanding? Maybe even a shrink? (*Little laugh*) I *could* just let him drive me home. Then I'd say something like . . . "The next time you feel you have to say 'I love you' to someone, say it to yourself and see if you believe it!" No, that'd go over his head. I think it went over mine. (*Another little laugh*) Of course I could just leave him waiting out there in the cold. Just slip out the back and really cross him out of my life. That way I'd be over him in a few more months. Give or take a few more friends. I don't know. I don't know. 'Cause if we do start in again, who'd say he won't keep this shit up? Right? I don't know. Maybe that's what I want. Maybe he's treating me just the way I want him to. Maybe I use him to give me that tragic torch-singer status that I admire so in others. If that's true . . . then he's my International Stud. Wouldn't that be a kick in the rubber parts? I love him. That's for sure. (*Fighting back tears*) But do I love him enough? What's enough? This is enough. (*Standing, chin up, confronting the audience*) Enough. (*Slow fade to black*)

THE END

FUGUE IN A NURSERY

FUGUE IN A NURSERY *premiered at La Mama E.T.C. on February 1,*
1979, with the following cast:

LAUREL	Marilyn Hamlin
ED	Edward D. Griffith
ALAN	Christopher Marcantel
ARNOLD	Harvey Fierstein

Directed by Eric Concklin
Music by Ada Janik
Stage Design by Bill Stabile
Lighting by Charles Embry
Production Stage Manager: Richard Jakiel

The production was subsequently presented by Mitchell Maxwell at the Orpheum Theatre with Maria Cellario as LAUREL, Will Jeffries as ED, and with lighting by Cheryl Thacker.

A NOTE ON THE MUSIC
A full score for Clarinet, French Horn, Violin, and Cello was created for the original production by Ada Janik. The music should never overshadow or cause melodramatic effect. Rather it is meant to harmonize the themes and clarify the moments. In Ms. Janik's original score each character was represented by an instrument: Arnold by the Cello, Alan by the Clarinet, Laurel by the Violin, and Ed by the French Horn. The musical notations of the text corresponded to the ones of the score.

CHARACTERS

ED

LAUREL: Thirty-five. Rather unfancy in appearance. Thoughtful and bright, though she shows a girlish enthusiasm.

ALAN: Eighteen. Shamefully beautiful. A frightened child in hustler's clothing.

ARNOLD

TIME

One year after the action of THE INTERNATIONAL STUD.

PLACE

Arnold's apartment and various rooms of Ed's farmhouse. Only one set is used (see description after prologue).

> ### IMPORTANT:
> In reading this script, it is imperative that close attention be paid to stage directions and character names, as the text may become unclear without that information.

PROLOGUE

There will be no preshow music, and the stage should be curtained. (For the La Mama production a revolving stage was used to hide the set from the entering audience.) As the houselights dim we hear a telephone ringing. During the following conversation (which should be tape-recorded), the audience sees the musicians entering the pit and hears them warming up their instruments. Simultaneously, slides are shown on a screen over the set. We see photos of Arnold in drag, Arnold and Ed walking and talking together, Ed and Laurel in similar leisure pastimes, and finally Arnold and Alan together. A telephone rings three times. (A loud radio in the background)

ARNOLD: Happy Home for the Bewildered.

LAUREL: Hello? Is this Arnold?

ARNOLD: That's what they tell me.

LAUREL: Hi. I don't know where to start. We've never met . . .

ARNOLD: Sounds like my life story. Hang on a second, would you? (*Muffled slightly*) HEY! Could you turn that thing down?

ALAN (*Far-off*): Who is it?

ARNOLD: I don't know, but if you'd turn that *fakaktah* thing down, I'd find out!

ALAN: If it's Murray, tell him I wanna speak to him. (*The radio noises fade out.*)

ARNOLD (*Syrupy*): Hello. You still there?

LAUREL: Look, am I interrupting something?

ARNOLD: Nothing you'd wanna write home about. (*Sound of a toilet flushing*) Well, come on. Speak up. I'm a drag queen not a mind reader.

LAUREL (*Flustered*):   Well, like I said, you don't know me but we have a mutual friend. Ed Reiss.

ARNOLD (*Pause*):   Is that what you called to tell me?

LAUREL: No. I'd better start again. You and I have never met. But, I think you'll know who I am. My name's Laurel. Ed and I live together. We're . . . lovers. As you know, Ed has a farm upstate where we spend the weekends and our vacations. Anyway, we got to talking and thought it'd be nice to have you up to visit for a few days. Still with me?

ARNOLD: I'm way ahead of you! I'm sorry, but I'm not into any of that kinky stuff.

LAUREL (*Laughing*):   That wasn't our intention at all. I just thought you might like to get out of the city for a few days. Ed's told me so much about you and I've wanted to meet you for the longest time . . .

ARNOLD: Whose idea was this?

LAUREL: We'd both like you to come.

ARNOLD: Yeah, but whose idea was this?

LAUREL: What's the difference? The point is, I know how much Ed values your friendship and that the two of you haven't seen that much of each other lately, which probably has to do with you and I not knowing each other, but hopefully this weekend will straighten all of that out. So, what do you say?

ARNOLD: I don't think so. I appreciate the invite, it was swell of you to call, but I don't think it's such a good idea. But look, maybe after the summer you and I could get together for lunch or something . . .

ALAN (*Mumbled and muffled*):   Wait a minute, I wanna go.

ARNOLD: Hang on a second, would you? (*Muffled conversation*) Listen, Laurel, do you think it'd be all right to bring a friend?

LAUREL: Of course. Please do. I'm sorry I didn't extend an

invitation to your friend myself, but Ed didn't tell me you were seeing anyone.

ARNOLD: He doesn't know about Alan.

LAUREL: Well, by all means bring him. That'll make the weekend nicer still; to have the both of you. So, we'll pick you up on the Friday train.

ARNOLD: No. We'll be driving up. Alan can borrow a car.

LAUREL: Great. Let me give you the directions.

ARNOLD: That's all right. I think I can remember how to get there.

LAUREL (*Loaded*): Of course, you've been here before. So, we'll see you Friday. I can hardly wait.

ARNOLD: Okay. See you then.

LAUREL: Bye-bye. (*Sound of phones clicking off*)

As the taped conversation ends, a slide appears on the screen:

NURSERY: a fugue

The conductor raises the baton and the first music begins to play. The set is an eight-foot-by-nine-foot heavily raked bed. It is mounded with pillows, blankets, and all the props needed in the course of the play. It will serve as all rooms in the house. The couples will be lighted as separately as possible, using color to indicate the pairings when the more complicated conversations begin. Special care should be taken that the four characters never appear to be in bed together. The desired effect is vulnerability, not obscenity.

As the music begins, the lights reveal Laurel filing her nails and Ed reading a newspaper. The other couple should not be seen. The music ends. . . .

LAUREL (*With deep satisfaction*): Isn't this civilized? (*Pause*) Do you think they have enough blankets? Maybe I should . . .

ED (*Sharply*): They'll be fine.

LAUREL: But it gets awfully cold . . .

ED *(Final)*:   Laurel, they'll be fine.

LAUREL: All right. Don't be so grouchy. *(Cuddling)* Wanna . . . ?

ED: Aren't you tired at all?

LAUREL: I'm too excited about having them here. Don't you wanna . . . ?

ED: Didn't you say you had some paperwork to do?

LAUREL *(Grabbing away his paper)*:   You're an old fart, you know that?

ED: Where's that newspaper?

LAUREL *(Handing it back. Bubbling.)*:   This is just so civilized! Guests up to our country home for the weekend. I can't tell you how excited I am.

ED: We *have* had guests before.

LAUREL: I'd hardly compare this to having your sister and her kids or your parents or even friends from school up. Imagine being hostess to your lover's ex and his new boyfriend. Now, if that isn't civilized, then what is? It's downright Noel Coward. How's your English accent?

ED: What?

LAUREL: It might be fun to use English accents all weekend.

ED: Would you stop.

LAUREL: What're you being so grouchy about? I'm just fooling around. *(Teasing)* Are my domestic fantasies making you nervous? Don't worry. I promise I won't propose to you.

ED: Very funny.

LAUREL: What is your problem?

ED: I don't see why they can't spend a few quiet days up here without all this rigmarole.

LAUREL: I'm excited. That's all.

ED: . . . because this is not the weekend that I had planned.

LAUREL: I have no idea what you're talking about.

ED (*Tossing off the newspaper*):   Alan. That's what I'm talking about.

LAUREL: What about him? He seems really nice.

ED: I should've known Arnold would pull something like this.

LAUREL: Now, look, I told you that Arnold asked me if he could bring a friend and that I told him he could.

ED: You had no right to. . . . This weekend was supposed to be just the three of us.

LAUREL: So what's the big deal? We've got enough food for four. I didn't have to open another room or anything. What'd you expect Arnold to do? Sit around with us all day, then watch us toddle off to bed while he slept alone? It's better this way. You'll see.

ED: No, you'll see. Did you catch the way he fawned over him at dinner? He practically cut his steak for him.

LAUREL: No more than I fawned over you. (*Cuddling*) And I did cut your steak.

ED (*Pouting*):   I could've killed you for that.

LAUREL: You're being ridiculous. There are bound to be compensations on all four of our parts. After all, the two of you were lovers. So little games and jealousies are bound to pop up. But I'm positive it's going to be a great weekend.

ED: Did you see how he made such a point of running off to bed early? "Oh, I'm so tired. All that good food has done me in." His hands all over the boy.

LAUREL: Well, if I had something as pretty as that to go to bed with, I wouldn't stay up late either.

ED (*Seriously considering*):   You think he's pretty?

LAUREL (*Baiting*):   Uh-huh.

ED: I don't like them that young.

LAUREL: I do. (*No reaction*) They make a nice couple. Don't you think? (*No answer*) I think Arnold's a very handsome man. Don't know why he'd want to put on a dress.

ED: You really like them that young?

LAUREL: What?

ED: As young as Alan.

LAUREL (*Considering*):   Sure. Why not? All that energy. Did you hear the way their bedsprings were squeaking?

ED: I think I do pretty well in the squeaking department.

LAUREL (*Teasing*):   You do, huh?

ED (*Moving closer*):   Well, making certain allowances for wear and tear . . .

LAUREL: It's too early in the race to make a plea for sympathy.

ED: You want to race? (*Excited*) All right, we'll race. And may the best man win.

LAUREL: And now, ladies and gentlemen, in the center ring, driving a 1968 Serta Orthopedic . . . Couple Number Two . . .

ED: Hey, no tickling before the gun.

LAUREL: On your marks. . . . Get set. . . . Go!

The lights quickly black out on them and snap on for Alan. He sits straight up in the bed as if frightened out of sleep by a bad dream. A slide appears:

SUBJECT

He takes a deep breath, relaxing a bit, then looks for Arnold, who is hidden under the mountain of blankets. He finds him asleep.

ALAN (*Shoving his face into Arnold's*):   Hello.

ARNOLD (*Asleep*):   If you can't say something nice, don't say nothin' at all. (*He rolls over.*)

ALAN (*Climbing over to the other side*):   Get your fat ass out of bed and get me something to eat. I'm hungry.

ARNOLD: Talk dirty to me.

ALAN: What? . . . Are you asleep?

ARNOLD (*Opening his eyes wide*):   God, you're gorgeous. (*Rolling away*) Now, go away.

ALAN: Come on, wake up.

ARNOLD: But I'm having this flawless dream.

ALAN: About me?

ARNOLD: If it is, will you let me go back to sleep?

ALAN: Yes.

ARNOLD: It's all about you.

ALAN (*Moving in close*):   What about me?

ARNOLD (*Feeling behind*):   My God, you really are awake.

ALAN: That doesn't matter.

ARNOLD (*Waking more fully*):   Maybe not to you . . .

ALAN: Stop changing the subject.

ARNOLD (*Attacking*):   Waste not, want not.

ALAN: Tell me the dream. (*Holding him off*)

ARNOLD: If you like it can we? . . .

ALAN: No.

ARNOLD (*Rolling over*):   Then I'm going back to sleep.

ALAN: Then I'm going to see if anyone else is up.

ARNOLD: Give my best to the bisexuals.

ALAN: Only he's bisexual. She's straight.

ARNOLD: How do you know?

ALAN: She told me so.

ARNOLD: Too bad. Mixed marriages never work.

ALAN: Yeah, then what were you doing with him?

ARNOLD: Slumming.

ALAN (*Climbing on top of him*):   And what're you doing with me?

ARNOLD: Nothing. It's gone.

ALAN: It'll be back.

ARNOLD (*Sulking*):   But it won't be the same.

ALAN: Of course it will.

ARNOLD: Do you ever think before you speak?

ALAN: No. Do you?

ARNOLD: Frequently. It passes the time while you're speaking.

ALAN: Be nice.

ARNOLD: Go back to sleep and wake up horny.

ALAN: You still haven't told me your dream.

ARNOLD: Why'd you wanna come up here this weekend?

ALAN: What's this black shit on the pillow?

ARNOLD: What black shit on the pillow?

ALAN: This black shit on the pillow.

ARNOLD: It's black shit on the pillow.

ALAN: Bullshit.

ARNOLD: Bullshit, black shit, why'd you wanna come?

ALAN: What do you mean?

ARNOLD: Never mind. Talk dirty to me.

ALAN: Tell me the dream.

ARNOLD: I ain't tellin' you nothin'. You lied to me.

ALAN: About what?

ARNOLD: You said it would come back. What's it waiting for?

ALAN: It's waiting to hear the dream.

ARNOLD (*Peeking under the covers*):   Is it really into that sort of
stuff?

ALAN: We're waiting.

ARNOLD: How old are you?

ALAN: You know how old I am.

ARNOLD: Tell me again, I need reassurance.

ALAN: The dream?

ARNOLD: I know who you are. You're the son I always avoided
having. Why's the lamp on?

ALAN: It's still dark out.

ARNOLD: Is there a storm?

ALAN: No, the sun's not up yet.

ARNOLD: You woke me in the middle of the night again?

ALAN: Do you mind?

ARNOLD: Of course not. (*Taking the boy into his arms like a child*)
Come on. What frightened you?

ALAN: Nothing. I just felt like talking.

ARNOLD: Comfortable?

ALAN: Tighter. Did Ed ever have bad dreams?

ARNOLD: Everyone does.

ALAN: Did you have to hold him?

ARNOLD: Talk dirty to me.

ALAN: Get me a dog.

ARNOLD: Why?

ALAN: I want one.

ARNOLD: I don't give you things.

ALAN: Yes you do. (*Arnold stiffens.*) No you don't. But, a dog's not a thing.

ARNOLD: All the more reason.

ALAN: C'mon, get me a dog.

ARNOLD: I have no money for a dog.

ALAN: You can get one at the pound. They're free.

ARNOLD: Then get one yourself.

ALAN: I will. Can I keep it at your place?

ARNOLD: You shouldn't wear cologne. It tastes terrible.

ALAN: Sometimes they have dogs up for adoption in the paper. Where's that other copy of the *Voice*?

ARNOLD: Under the bed. (*Alan starts for it.*) No, don't move. I want to remember me like this forever.

ALAN: I want a cigarette anyway.

ARNOLD (*Sulking*):   Is that what you tell the other models at the studio; that I buy you things and that's why you live with me?

ALAN: No. Of course not.

ARNOLD: You make more money modeling for an hour than I do in a week. I don't buy you things. Don't say I do.

ALAN: I don't.

ARNOLD: Good. 'Cause I don't. Not things. Cigarettes. That's all.

ALAN: All right already. Want a cigarette?

ARNOLD: They're mine, aren't they?

ALAN: Then do you mind if I have one?

ARNOLD: That's why they're here. Don't do that to yourself; treat yourself like a piece of meat. It's what all them leering faggots do, so you don't have to do it to yourself.

ALAN (*Lighting a cigarette*):   I don't.

ARNOLD: At least stop enjoying it. You don't have to be a model.

ALAN: You don't have to be a drag queen.

ARNOLD: How ridiculous! They're not the same things at all.

ALAN: What's the difference?

ARNOLD: A model IS. A drag queen . . . aspires.

ALAN: Great aspirations!

ARNOLD: Very funny. I'm serious, Alan. Fantasies are fine in the bedroom, but outside they're not fantasies, they're lies.

ALAN: What are you talking about?

ARNOLD: Your hustler trips.

ALAN (*Stuffs cigarette in Arnold's mouth*):   Would you stop? Where's that newspaper?

ARNOLD (*Handing it over*):   Here.

ALAN (*Long look at Arnold*):   I love you.
   (*Arnold rolls into Alan's arms as the lights fade down on them and up on Laurel and Ed. They are in each other's arms.*)

LAUREL: I don't believe I've seen you this turned on in months. If that's Arnold's effect on you, then I think I'll ask him to move in.

ED: It's not Arnold, it's you.

LAUREL: Is that why you called me Arnold?

ED: I did not.

LAUREL (*Giggling*): Oh yes you did. Deep into loving, you whispered into my ear, "I love you, Arnold."

ED: That's not funny. You shouldn't make up things like that.

LAUREL: I'm not. What're you getting so upset about? Minds wander during sex. It's like dreaming; all sorts of things pass through the mind. I once blurted out the phone number of the house I grew up in. I'm not upset you called me Arnold, so there's no reason for you to be.

ED: I never called you Arnold. That's something passing in *your* mind.

LAUREL: All right. So I misheard you. Take it easy.

ED: It's that damned kid. This was going to be a beautiful weekend. The three of us together. I thought . . . that having the two of you here together . . . that I'd be able to put a period on that whole section of my life. But the second he walked through the door I knew that I'd put the period there long ago and this whole weekend was unnecessary.

LAUREL: Well, thanks a lot. I'm glad you've made up your mind.

ED: That's not what I meant. I wasn't planning on comparing the two of you. Christ! Everything was going to be so simple, I wanted us all to be friends. Then Arnold had to bring that kid.

LAUREL: He also brought a cake, a lace tablecloth, and *The Village Voice*. (*Handing him the paper*) Enjoy them all.

ED (*Trying to cuddle*): Come here and I'll read you the funny pages.

LAUREL: I have my own reading, thank you.

(*She picks up some papers as the lights cross back to Arnold and Alan in each other's arms.*)

ARNOLD: Feels so strange. I can't get over it; you and I in this room with them in there. This was my room, y'know. I mean, we slept together in there but I kept my clothes in here in case any neighbors or family dropped in and peeked around. He didn't want them to think we were queer or anything. I can't believe I put up with that.

ALAN: So, what do you think?

ARNOLD: About what?

ALAN: Ed. Seeing him again with me to compare him to.

ARNOLD: Is that what I'm supposed to be doing?

ALAN: Sure. I have.

ARNOLD: So, what do you think?

ALAN: He ain't so hot. Not hot enough to be "The Great Love of Your Life" anyway.

ARNOLD: I don't consider him "The Great Love of My Life." But he's got his good points. He's good-natured, good-looking, good in bed . . .

ALAN: . . . good and boring.

ARNOLD: He's not good and boring. He's just plain boring. But there's worse things to be. I once knew this guy who . . .

ALAN: There's a lot of that going around.

ARNOLD: Hey, who's the straight man here?

ALAN: I'm at that impressionable age. You're rubbing off on me.

ARNOLD (*Blanche du Bois*):   I never touched the Gray boy.

ALAN (*Laughs*):   Feel better?

ARNOLD: Yeah. So anyway, I once knew this guy . . .

ALAN: Did you really love Ed?

ARNOLD: I guess so.

ALAN: And he loved you.

ARNOLD: I wouldn't say that.

ALAN: I would. I see how he looks at you. Why'd you two break up?

ARNOLD: We wanted different things.

ALAN: Like what?

ARNOLD: I wanted a husband and he wanted a wife.

ALAN: You ever think of going back with him?

ARNOLD: You can't go back.

ALAN: Why not?

ARNOLD: Because.

ALAN: Because why?

ARNOLD: Because . . . because . . . because   people   change. They're never the same twice. So how can you go back?

ALAN: Well, did you ever want to start out fresh again?

ARNOLD: Jesus Christ! Were you ever not true to form? Thank God I was not your mother. I could have denied you nothing. I am in awe of her that she denied you as much as she did for you to need to ask for so much now.

ALAN: When I said that I loved you before, you didn't answer me.

ARNOLD: I didn't realize that it was a question.

ALAN: Well?

ARNOLD: Here, read the newspaper. (*Throws it at him*) (*Alan rolls away*) Are you pouting? This child is unbelievable. Come, I'll read to you. Okay? Okay.

A slide appears on the screen:

CODETTA

The lights come up on Laurel and Ed reading the paper in the same position as the other couple. Both couples are visible, but the separation is clear.

ED (*Reading from the paper*):   Banes, Iowa. "That'll teach them folks not to mess around with true love," beamed eighty-year-old Sarah Fonedwell as she left the Iowa courtroom arm in arm with her fifteen-year-old boyfriend.

Miss Fonedwell was charged with statutory rape and impairing the morals of a minor after the young boy's parents learned that their son was having intimate relations with the great-grandmother of six. The couple had met when the boy took over a friend's paper route. Miss Fonedwell was a steady customer. Judge John Sirrocco dismissed the charges saying, "No real harm was done. It's all in the boy's education." But before adjourning court, he shook a warning finger at the feisty lady, saying, "From now on you'd better walk to the corner when you want a paper." To which she quipped, "I don't mind the added exercise, but I sure will miss them home deliveries." (*The couples keep the integrity of their pairing while building in rhythm.*)

LAUREL: You made me stop working to listen to that?

ED: I think it's very funny. Don't you?

ARNOLD: That's disgusting.

LAUREL: Would you think it was so funny if it had been an eighty-year-old man seducing a fifteen-year-old girl? You think the judge would have said it was all in her education?

ED: But it wasn't.

ALAN: I don't know, I think it's kind of sexy.

LAUREL: Sexy?

ED: Yeah, sure. Imagine his feeling of power. The strength he must have felt: he, young and virile; she, old and withered, drinking in his youth. . . .

ALAN: Think of the pleasure he gave her. I bet she even thought she was fifteen again.

LAUREL: You see him as the giver and her as the taker? That's even more perverse than I'd imagined it. I saw her giving her last favor; passing on her last gift to the next generation. But you see it as a simple matter of lust.

ED: Well, if you'd listened to the way she talked, you'd see she's obviously just a dirty old lady.

ARNOLD: I can't believe that anyone would be that self-destructive. I mean, if she was eighty to begin with, how old was she when it was over?

ALAN: Obviously, she was rejuvenated in his arms. A miracle of modern sex.

ARNOLD: The only miraculous thing about modern sex is that it exists.

LAUREL: Did you ever sleep with someone then wonder who gave more; or who enjoyed it more?

ARNOLD: Could we change the subject?

ALAN (*Pushing Arnold away*):   They don't buy the milk if they can get the cow for free.

ARNOLD: That's what I like to hear: Good old American "not now."

LAUREL: At the risk of rendering you impotent for the remainder of "The Milkman's Matinee," could you make love to me if I was an eighty-year-old woman and you a fifteen-year-old boy?

ALAN: Fierce, passionate love.

ARNOLD: Ah, but would I make love to you?

ED: Why not?

LAUREL: You could really sleep with an eighty-year-old woman?

ED: Are we talking about me or me if I was fifteen?

ALAN: At least she was willing to give it a go.

ED: I give what I can and trust that it's enough.

ALAN: Not unless you can slip in a few one-liners.

ED: I don't lie awake nights wondering whether I gave more or you gave more or about how old you are or if you're pretty or not. And yes, I could probably make love to an eighty-year-old woman. I could make love to an eighty-year-old camel. I could probably make love to anything . . . as long as it kept its mouth shut.
       (*The lights go out on Laurel and Ed.*)

ALAN: Shhhhhhh! (*Listening*) I thought I heard someone talking.

ARNOLD: It was probably Ed talking in his sleep.

ALAN: He talks in his sleep?

ARNOLD: Talks, screams, gnashes his teeth, kicks . . .

ALAN: Really? How'd you ever get any sleep?

ARNOLD: I never slept better.

ALAN: You really loved him, huh?

ARNOLD: We starting that again?

ALAN: I'm just curious. Why?

ARNOLD: Wha'd'ya mean, "Why?" Why does anyone love anyone? Because I did. Because . . . I did. Because . . . he let me.

A slide appears on the screen:

STRETTO

Alan appears alone in a light as Arnold and Ed prepare for the scene. During this section both Alan and Laurel will appear in their own lights regardless to whom they speak. Arnold and Ed will appear center stage together.

ALAN: I'm not talking to you. Deserting me all afternoon like that. Where the hell did the two of you disappear to anyway?

ARNOLD: We spent the afternoon in bed. Jealous?

ALAN: Why should I be? You didn't do anything.

ARNOLD: How do you know? We were alone for three hours.

LAUREL: If you say you only talked, then I believe you. Though I can't say I understand why you had to do it in bed.

ARNOLD: You remember that poem about sleep: That in sleep all men are equal, the pauper and the king and all that?

ED: Something about there being no limitations on dreams?

ARNOLD: Yeah, that's the one. Well, I figure if everyone's equal in sleep then just lying down makes you at least reachable. Besides, that's where I do my best thinking. Don't have to worry about the body, it just relaxes, leaving all the blood for the brain.

ED: I used to call your bedroom the Nursery, remember? It was always so warm and comfortable and safe.

ARNOLD: I thought it was because we never went to bed without a bottle.

ED: And you saved every bottle we drank together. You still have them?

ARNOLD: Nah.

ED: You said you wanted to make something out of them.

ARNOLD: When we broke up I did. Quite a racket. (*Mimes throwing bottles*) And quite a mess. So tell me, what's new with you?

ED: Not much.

ARNOLD: Well, are you seeing anyone? (*Ed laughs.*) That wasn't supposed to be funny. You have been known to sidestep on occasion.

ED: Not since we've been together.

ARNOLD: Give it time.

ED: I doubt it. I really do love her very much.

ARNOLD: I'm happy for you. What can I say? It's what you said you wanted and I'm glad it's working out.

ED: Are you jealous?

ARNOLD: No. Should I be?

ED: You don't love him.

ARNOLD: What's that got to do with anything.

ED: 'Cause I'm jealous of him anyway.

LAUREL (*To Alan*):   So, tell me about yourself.

ALAN (*To Arnold*):   I had to talk to her all afternoon. Nothing else to do with the two of you running off. Y'know she tried to make me? It's the truth. And not even me. I mean it wasn't me she was trying to make, particularly. She's just got this thing for faggots. It's true. Ask her. She'll tell you the whole story. I think she likes to tell the story as much as she likes to make the faggots. Anyway, she's proved you wrong. You said people only went after me because of my looks, but she went after me because of my likes.

ED (*With Arnold in his arms*):   This feels wonderful.

ALAN: You know, at first I was insulted; being wanted just because I'm gay. But, that's almost like being wanted for myself. . . . I think I'm flattered.

ARNOLD (*To Ed*):   Hey, watch your hands. I'm a married man.

LAUREL (*To Alan. They are now lighted together.*):   So, tell me about yourself.

ALAN: I'm a model. Clothes, toothpaste . . . anything they can sell with an All-American puss. I'd like to be an actor, but I think I'll let that ride until I've made all I can out of being the American Dream.

LAUREL: And what about your childhood?

ALAN: According to Arnold, it's only just begun.

LAUREL: Arnold really is something else. You two must be very happy together.

ALAN: Believe me, there are easier things than living with Arnold. He thinks it's immoral, that it makes him a lesser person to love me because I'm good-looking.

LAUREL: Oh, come on.

ALAN: No, really. He'd be much happier if I was his age, his size, his . . . size. Sometimes I'm not sure if he wants a lover or a bookend.

LAUREL: It's good that you have a sense of humor. Ed has none. But that's part of his charm.

ALAN: No wonder they didn't last.

LAUREL: Well, I think there's more to it than that. But I can't tell you how happy I am that Arnold has you. My reasons may be a little selfish. Y'know, they were still going together when I met Ed. I didn't know it, of course. If I did I never would have started seeing Ed. See, I met him through a friend from group . . .

ALAN: Group? Like in therapy group?

LAUREL: That's right. It's kind of a story, I guess. I had just come through a rather bad affair with a guy who turned out to be bisexual. (The bi leaning toward his new boyfriend.)

When he broke the news to me, I was quite a mess. See, he wasn't the first man to pull that on me. All told there were three of that particular persuasion plus a pair of married men thrown in for good measure. Not the greatest track record for a "One-Man Woman" type like myself. I became what you could call . . . depressed. And when I looked among my friends for a sympathetic ear I realized that every one of them was gay. That's when it began to dawn on me that I might just have gotten myself into a rut. So, off to therapy I went. That's where I met Janet, who told me about a handsomely available teacher she knew named Ed. She set up the get-together and that was that.

ALAN: A real live blind date. How exotic.

LAUREL (*Amused*): Blind indeed. We'd been dating for over a month before he ever told me about Arnold. But by then, it was too late to pull out without a fight.

ALAN: So you fought?

LAUREL: No, that's not what I meant. I mean, it wasn't a fight. I just pulled back enough to let Ed feel his freedom: No promises, no pressure, no commitments. Soon he was telling me that he wanted to end his relationship with Arnold. So, I suggested he speak to my therapist and he joined the group. . . .

ARNOLD: You never told me about the shrink.

ED: Because I know how you feel about "Shrinks." But really, the group's been very supportive. They've never pushed me toward any decision that I didn't want to make.

ARNOLD: Now I know where all that "I owe myself the chance to lead a normal life" bullshit came from. So, I suppose you're straight now?

ED: Not now. I always have been.

ARNOLD: And me? . . . And all the others, what were we—a phase you were going through?

ED (*Laughing*): You always were a homosexual chauvinist. To you everyone's either gay or in the closet.

ARNOLD: What's sex like with her?

ED: It's very beautiful.

ARNOLD: Is it satisfying?

ED: I'm with her, aren't I?

ARNOLD: So, what does that mean? I could've kept you. You don't believe it, but it's true. I've done a lot of thinking about you and some of the others I've been through and I think I've found a pattern: When things get too good . . . I get out. Well, I guess to a degree we all do. But most pull out; ride off into the sunset with a wave and a wink and a "Hi-yo, Silver!" But not me. I am a pusher. I nudge and *kvetch* and cry and demand until I leave my partner no possible alternative but for him to run for his life. That makes him the villain and leaves the victim role to me. And "Poor Pearl" is a role I really love to play.

ED: I never saw myself the villain.

ARNOLD: You never saw yourself period.

ED: I wouldn't have stayed. In the year that Laurel and I have been seeing each other I haven't once fooled around. And believe me, our relationship allows for that. No, I wouldn't have stayed. (*Thinks*) I bet you think you could get me back if you wanted to.

ARNOLD: I don't want to. That's precisely my point. Why waste all that energy? When an affair hits the skids you shed it like last year's fashion and head back to the streets. There are plenty more where that one came from. And that, my ex-husband, is what I call the miracle of modern sex.

LAUREL: We attend private sessions on Tuesdays and on Thursdays we have group. You and Arnold should try it. Maybe not the private sessions but a group's the ideal way to open up the lines of communication between two people and really solidify a relationship.

ALAN: Sounds inspiring.

ED: And what about you? You don't love that kid.

ARNOLD: You said that, not me.

ED: So, do you?

ARNOLD: Maybe. What makes you think I'm in love with anyone?

ED: Because we've been lying in bed together for over an hour
in and out of each other's arms and you've yet to make a pass
at me.

ARNOLD: That's not love. That's good taste.

ED: Come on, Arnold, who is it? No, let me guess . . . could it
be me?

ARNOLD (*Jumping*):   God, the EGO!!!!

ED (*Pulling him back*):   I was only kidding.

ARNOLD: You wouldn't know him anyway. I don't know him.
Not really.

ED: You wouldn't love him if you did.

ARNOLD: You're really impossible.

ED (*Genuine*):   Who is he?

ARNOLD: Well, you know The International Stud bar has this
dark backroom where everyone goes to fool around. . . . What
am I telling you for? I wouldn't know about such things if it
wasn't for you showing them to me. Anyway, I've been going
there a lot lately. Two, three times a week.

ED: What does Alan have to say about that?

ARNOLD (*Sarcastically*):   We have a very honest and open relationship. So, there's this guy there that I meet every night and
we always get it on together. We haven't talked about anything
really and we meet there only by chance. I mean, we haven't
set it up that way or anything. It's just that he's always there

waiting for me, or if I get there first I wait for him. . . . Oh, never mind.

ED: No, go on, it sounds very romantic.

ARNOLD: Just forget it, all right?

ED: I'm sorry, but first you tell me you're in love. Then you tell me you can only get it on in a backroom. . . .

ARNOLD: That's not it at all.

ED: Have you ever made love together alone?

ARNOLD: No, but . . .

ED: Have you ever had a drink together in the light of the front room?

ARNOLD: He's very shy.

ED (*Laughing*):   Arnold, I think you've reached a new plateau of perversity.

ARNOLD: Hey, wait a minute here, who gospeled to whom about the advantages of the backroom. I'd never seen a backroom until after you. . . .

ED: I never took you into one.

ARNOLD: But that's where you would rather have taken me. If we'd met and stayed in the backroom we never would have had the problems we did.

ED: Is that your answer now? Put the blame on me. "Ed, you hurt me so bad. I'll never trust to love again." So, you're going to play this one nice and safe.

ARNOLD: Look who's knocking safety! Mr. All-American Heterosexual! Locked your life up tight, didn't you. Picked yourself a nice little wifey type, plain and lonely enough to never worry about her stepping out on you, pleasant and giving enough to boss her around to get her to do anything or go anywhere that you want. And you're gonna read my beads? (*Arnold makes a dive under the covers.*)

ED: Hey! What are you doing?

ARNOLD (*Emerging at the foot of the bed next to Ed's feet, his feet next to Ed's face*): Take it easy. I'm just looking for a second opinion.

ED: I thought you were trying to get to the bottom of me.

ARNOLD: Heterosexuality has done *nada* for your wit. Your feet stink.

ED: They weren't expecting company.

ARNOLD (*Picking up a bottle*): What's this?

ED: My cologne.

ARNOLD (*Sniffing*): What is it, "Ben-Hur"? (*Sprinkles it about*) Now I'm in my element. Toss me a pillow. (*Ed does.*) Thanks. And just what's wrong with playing it safe? I can sleep when I want, eat when I want, fuck when I want . . .

ED: . . . want when you want.

ARNOLD: Cheap shot.

ED: Can I just ask you a question? If you don't love Alan, why do you stay with him?

ARNOLD: He needs me.

ED: Come on.

ARNOLD: All right, I need him.

ED: Forget I asked.

ARNOLD: What the hell would you know about need? You're like a baby in a crib, hands and fingers flexing, "Gimme. Gimme." You're all want. So, maybe I don't love him, but I need that gorgeous imbecile and I like to think that he needs me.

ED: So, he's like a pet.

ARNOLD: You're a pig, you know that?

ED: Arnold, I am exhausted from trying to understand.

ARNOLD: It gets easier with practice. He ain't complaining.

ED: Don't you think he deserves to be loved?

ARNOLD: Of course he does. Who doesn't? But, who is?

ED: I am.

ARNOLD: What do you suppose it is that makes me want to shove a chair up your nose? (*Pause*) What the hell am I supposed to do: sit around crying over losing you?

ED: That's not what I meant. I'm very happy you have him, all right?

ARNOLD (*Long pause*):   You and Laurel working on having kids yet?

ED: We haven't really discussed it in detail.

ARNOLD: Don't you still want kids?

ED: Still? Who said anything about having kids?

ARNOLD: You did. Don't you remember? At the party there was that woman who arranged for gay couples to adopt. You probably don't remember, you said you wanted a boy, but you were gay then.

ED: I remember. But that was just talk. You know, a fantasy.

ARNOLD: Is that what it was?

ED: Sure, like our airplane, and our island . . .

ARNOLD: . . . and our relationship.

ED: That was one of the things that made me love you: that I could fantasize about anything, let my mind go as far out as it could, and there you were, all caught up in the dream with me, making it almost real.

ARNOLD: 'Cause I didn't know it wasn't. Those things weren't fantasies to me. To me a fantasy is a Genie or a magic lamp, something impossible that you wouldn't really want even if you could have it. Our airplane, our island, our child . . . they

weren't fantasies. They were possibilities. None of it was impossible. Y'know, I keep a ledger where I list things like that. And when I get an item that's on the list, I put a check mark next to it. The ledger's got more than one hundred pages filled with my possibilities. You'd be surprised how many check marks there are too. Oh, they're little things like an electric toothbrush, or an azalea bush, or a subscription to *National Geographic*. But they each mark an achievement for me.

ED: What's the inflation ratio—items as opposed to check marks?

ARNOLD: Never counted.

ED: Am I on the list?

ARNOLD: Listed and checked off.

ED: That's cheating. You don't have me.

ARNOLD (*Cocksure*):   Don't I?

ED: No.

ARNOLD: I'll be sure to correct my ledger first thing Monday morning.

ED (*Pause*):   Tell me something, what would you do with a subscription to *National Geographic*?

ARNOLD (*Hiding his insult*):   Look at the dirty pictures.

ED (*Agreeing*):   Oh.

Arnold pulls a pillow over his head in disgust as a slide appears on the screen:

COUNTER SUBJECT

Arnold and Alan are in each other's arms, just waking. The other two remain in the dark until indicated.

LAUREL (*Calling out*):   Hurry up, you two sleepyheads, breakfast is on the table.

ARNOLD: Sleepyheads?

ALAN (*Ecstatic*):   Breakfast? How'd you sleep?

ARNOLD: Awfully. I dreamt that I was walking down this twist-ing path and no matter how carefully I watched I kept stepping in cowpies. . . .

ALAN: You mean cowchips. Not pies. Chips.

ARNOLD: Whatever. Anyway, as I turned a corner around this big Camperdown elm I saw Ed squatting down naked making the cowpies . . . or chips. Now, what the hell do you suppose that was supposed to mean?

ALAN: Maybe it was prophetic dreaming.

ARNOLD: Prophesying what?

ALAN: Maybe the toilet's gonna bust.

LAUREL (*Calling out*):   C'mon, you two. We'll be late for church.

ARNOLD: She say "Church"?

ALAN: Didn't you know, Ed plays organ for the services every Sunday morning.

ARNOLD: Give me a break. And they say dreams are mean-ingless?

LAUREL (*Now lighted*):   Aren't you two coming?

ARNOLD: Actually, Laurel, I'd love to go but my religion strictly forbids entering any church for other than historical purposes: looking at stained glass, et cetera.

LAUREL: Nonsense. I have lots of Jewish friends that visit churches.

ARNOLD: Oh, but I'm not Jewish anymore. I've converted. I'm what you'd call a Scientific American. Yes. See . . . we believe that all of mankind's problems can be solved with vitamins.

ALAN (*Under his breath*):   Groan!

LAUREL: So, you have no need for prayer.

ARNOLD: I wouldn't say that. I'm often found on my knees.

ALAN (*A bit louder*): Groan!

LAUREL: But if you can't enter a house of God, where do you pray?

ARNOLD: Harvard.

ALAN (*Loud*): Groan!!! (*Arnold leaps on him, laughing.*)

ED (*Lights on him and Laurel*): What's the matter?

LAUREL: Nothing. Are you ready?

ED: Are they coming down?

LAUREL: No. They're sleeping in.

ED: What's the matter? Did Arnold say something?

LAUREL: I'm not upset. Are you coming?

ED: This weekend's not turning out the way you thought it would either. Is it? Just remember, it was your idea.

LAUREL: I like Arnold. I really do. It's just . . . when I thought about this weekend I knew it was a setup for all sorts of competitions, comparisons . . . and I was ready for them. After all, I knew no matter what happened that I had you. I knew you'd made your choice between us and felt I could deal with anything knowing you had chosen me.

ED: That's what I've been saying all along.

LAUREL: Would you just listen? . . . That's not what's happening here. Arnold is so relaxed, as if he has nothing on his mind, like he's simply visiting friends for the weekend.

ED: What's wrong with that?

LAUREL: He's just too sure of himself. Like a kid all puffed up with a secret.

ED: Are you sorry they're here?

LAUREL: No. Just aware. (*Lights out on them*)

ALAN: You weren't very nice to her.

ARNOLD: I do have my limits, and one of them happens to be Sunday morning Mountain Church services. Actually, I'm shocked that Ed let her ask us at all. He probably would have introduced us as long-lost relatives. The charcoal-gray sheep of the family.

ALAN: Kissing cousins. So, what do you make of her?

ARNOLD: She's all right. A little too giving and gracious for my tastes, but deep down she's a survivor.

ALAN: How can you say that? She makes the same mistakes over and over.

ARNOLD: Once is a mistake. Twice a misfortunate coincidence. But three times and you can start writing your memoirs.

ALAN: He's number four.

ARNOLD: I wonder if maybe she's really gay? I know just the woman to bring her out too. Bet she'd make a great lesbian.

ALAN: And you'd make a great lamp.

ARNOLD: I'm afraid I'd make a great deal more than that.

ALAN (*Climbing onto him*):   I'll make do. . . .

Lights out on them as a slide appears on the screen:

STRETTO

Lights come up on all four, holding plates and napkins as if they've just finished lunch. They begin to pass the plates to Laurel.

ED: Laurel, that was a delicious lunch. Isn't she a great cook, Arnold? Besides being beautiful.

ARNOLD (*Snatching the pile of plates from Laurel*):   Just delicious. And beautiful.

ALAN: I bet I've gained five pounds in the past two days.

ARNOLD: Here, let me help you with those dishes.

LAUREL (*Grabbing the dishes back*): No, I'm fine. Ed, why don't you take Arnold and Alan out to the barn and show them our new canning machine. We've been canning all our own vegetables, you know.

ARNOLD: Really? Ed, why don't you take Alan and show it to him. He's the real can connoisseur in the family. I'll stay and help Laurel. We've yet to have a moment alone to compare notes on you.

ED: Just what Laurel's been waiting for.

LAUREL (*Embarrassed*): Ed!

ED (*Taking two glasses*): Let's hit the road before the fur starts flying. Grab that bottle of brandy. No need for us to rough it.

(*There is a sudden light change, focusing on Arnold and Alan in the center of the bed. Ed moves to the upstage right corner of the bed as Laurel moves with her dishes and dishrag to the downstage left corner. When Ed speaks, it is to Alan's next physical position.*)

ALAN: Go start packing. We're getting out of here tonight.

ARNOLD: Would you stop?

ALAN: I suppose you're going to tell me you spent another innocent afternoon in bed. Only this time with her.

ARNOLD: It was not an afternoon, it was only an hour. And we spent it in the kitchen doing dishes. You knew where we were. If you were lonely you should have come in.

ALAN: Oh, I wasn't lonely. I had lots of company. He tried to make me.

ARNOLD: Would you please . . .

ALAN: I'd like to be able to spend two minutes in this house without someone trying to shove me onto a couch . . .

ED: Would you like another brandy?

ALAN: . . . and you put down the studio? At least when someone makes a pass at me there, it's got a trip to Europe or a
movie contract as part of the deal. Here it's "Alone at last!"
and a dive for my zipper.

ED: Well, here we are: Alone at last.

ARNOLD: Alan, when we walk down the street and an old lady
asks you for the time, you swear she's trying to make you.
Now, I'd be the last to say you weren't irresistible, but, Angel,
there are limits. (*Joins Laurel*)

ED: We can sit on this haystack. (*Alan joins him.*)

ARNOLD (*Wiping a dish*):   Isn't this civilized? Doing the dishes.

LAUREL: Stuck with the dishes. I feel like we went out to lunch,
you thinking that I was treating and I thinking that you were
treating and here we are: working off the bill.

ARNOLD: No, I know, we're in-laws on one of them detergent
commercials.

LAUREL: "Why, Marge, your dishes are so shiny. I can see myself!"

ARNOLD: "Well, so can I!" Platter, platter on the stack. Does she
think I want him back? (*He winces a bit.*)

LAUREL: You work fast. I thought we'd kinda waltz around the
table a few times first.

ARNOLD: Sorry, I thought we might as well get it out of the
way.

LAUREL: So, do you?

ARNOLD: What do you think?

LAUREL: I think you do.

ARNOLD: Really. Why?

LAUREL: Well, you don't love Alan.

ARNOLD: I keep hearing that. What makes you think I don't love Alan?

LAUREL: How could you when you still love Ed?

ARNOLD: What makes you think I still love Ed?

LAUREL: Well, I know that from the start you loved Ed more than he loved you. . . .

ARNOLD: He told you that?

LAUREL: It's nothing to be ashamed of.

ARNOLD: Of course not. If it's true that one person always loves more than the other, why not be one who feels the most? But why would that make you think I'd want him back now?

LAUREL: You're here, aren't you?

ARNOLD: You asked me to come.

LAUREL: Still, you didn't have to. (*Uncomfortably*) Look, I know more about your relationship than you might think. We have few secrets and a great deal of openness. It's the kind of relationship we have. We share almost everything with complete freedom. . . . What I'm trying to say is that I know a great deal of what was said between you. . . .

ARNOLD: So?

LAUREL: Please. So, I know what it feels like to be in that position. You felt hurt, rejected, angry. . . . Then you started to wonder if there was ever anything between you. Or maybe you'd made it all up? Who's to blame for that? Who's to blame for breaking up?

ARNOLD: Are we talking about you or me?

LAUREL: You told Ed that you could get him back if you wanted to.

ARNOLD: I also told him that I didn't want to.

LAUREL: Then why do you call him all the time? I know about your calls in the afternoon while I'm at work.

ARNOLD: He told you that I call him?

LAUREL (*Haughty*):   I told you, we have a very honest relationship.

ARNOLD: Laurel, I don't want you to misunderstand and think I'm calling Ed a liar, but I've never called him. Yes, we've spoken on the phone, but he has always called me. And I've made those conversations as brief as was politely possible. He'd call and tell me all about how happy the two of you were and all about his family (none of whom I've ever met) and I'd say a nice little good-bye and that was that.

LAUREL: Then why'd you come up here?

ARNOLD: To see how my paint job was holding up. Y'know, I painted this room. Took me days. I was scared shitless of dripping on the floor; you know what a fussbudget Ed can be. . . .

LAUREL: I'm sorry. I have no right to talk to you this way. I'm pushing you to admit something that you're obviously not ready to face.

ARNOLD: You're pushing me all right! But I don't think you realize toward what. Laurel . . . are you happy with Ed?

LAUREL: The happiest I've ever been in my life.

ARNOLD: So what else do you want?

ALAN: To own a disco. (*Lights out on Arnold and Laurel, leaving Alan and Ed quite alone*) I knew this guy, he was a few years older than me, who'd met this older guy who set him up in business. I figured that I could do the same. But when I made my entrance into the Big Apple, and believe me, a blue-eyed blond of fourteen makes quite an entrance into any apple, I found that no one was interested in hearing about my business skills. In fact, no one was interested in anything much besides my price tag for an evening. See, people with tastes for blue-eyed blonds of fourteen are used to paying for it and consider a freebie suspicious, if not downright immoral. And so, I be-

came a hustler. I figured that I needed the affection more than they needed the money. Now, of course, things are different. But then . . . anyway, I got along. The hustling led to some connections, the connections to my career, and the career to . . .

ED: Arnold!

ALAN: No, Arnold was more of a detour.

ED: That's Arnold.

ALAN: One night, I went out drinking with a friend and got more than usually polluted. Somehow I ended up in a Lower East Side bar that had a drag show. Anyway, I wound up in a fight with this big black guy who threw me down on a table, jumped up on my chest, and put a knife to my neck. Everyone was screaming and crowding around to watch me get cut, when all of a sudden there was silence, and the crowd parted to make an aisle, and up through it like Moses through the Red Sea came this Amazon woman. You never seen anything like it. She was beautiful! Not like "pretty" beautiful, but like "mountain" beautiful. You know what I mean?

ED: That's Arnold!

ALAN: She put her hand out to the black guy like this, (*He demonstrates the gesture with haughty glare*) and he just handed over the knife and disappeared. No words, no nothing, just like that.

ED: When did you realize it was a guy?

ALAN: I was too drunk that night to realize that *I* was a guy. I sort of . . . fell onto that discovery the next morning.

ED (*Moving in closer*): How'd you feel about it?

ALAN: I'm with him, aren't I? (*Easing away. Holding up his glass.*) More, please. (*Ed pours.*) Now, you tell me about you. That's the whole reason we're here.

ED: Is it?

ALAN: Sure is. Arnold didn't want to come, but I wasn't going to let this chance to see my competition go by.

ED: I'm no competition. (*He moves closer again.*)

ALAN: Well, then, my predecessor. Stop changing the subject. Tell me about you.

ED: Why don't you ask Arnold to tell you. I'm sure he's got lots to say on the subject.

ALAN: He has.

ED: And?

ALAN: He says you're a self-centered, insensitive, boring fool who wouldn't know love if it wore wings, a diaper, and shot heart-shaped arrows at your butt.

ED: Meaning himself?

ALAN: Meaning himself. (*Lying down triumphantly*) Anything you'd care to add?

ED: No, that'll do. (*Lying down next to him*) And what do you think?

ALAN: I'll reserve my judgment until I can make a closer inspection.

ED (*Putting his arm around Alan*):   Close enough?

ALAN (*Sitting up quickly*):   Too close for comfort. You asked me to sit in the hay, not roll in it.

ED (*Coming up behind him*):   It was a two-part question. I think you're very beautiful.

ALAN: I thought you were reformed.

ED: I'm not proposing marriage to you. (*Gently pulling him back*) If you want me to stop just say so. Do you? (*No response*) I didn't think so.
    (*The lights go out on them immediately, leaving Arnold alone at the downstage right corner of the bed.*)

ARNOLD: I don't know when to stop. That's my problem. Me
and my fucking mouth. I didn't come up here to hurt her. I
didn't even come up here to hurt him. (Though that would've
been all right.) I was so proud of myself until now. I thought
I was really handling this whole situation so maturely. I guess
I was saving it all up for that. (*To Alan as if he were there*) I
hope you're enjoying all this.

ALAN (*From the dark*):   Oh, I am.

ARNOLD: Good. 'Cause it's all your fault. Couldn't take no for
an answer, you just had to come up here. Why couldn't I just
keep my trap shut? I've always thought of myself as a kind
person. Not saintly but generously thoughtful (in a bitchy sort
of way). But since being here, I have said nothing that hasn't
hurt someone: you, Ed, Laurel, myself. Well, she asked for it.
She begged for it . . . and boy, did I give it to her. I was bril-
liant. Point after pointless point, I proved beyond a shadow
of a doubt that Ed has no idea that she even exists. That, to
him, she's simply living proof of his normality.

ALAN (*Joining Arnold, they fold clothing into a suitcase.*):   How many
dishes did she break over your head?

ARNOLD: Not enough to keep me quiet.

ALAN: You elaborated?

ARNOLD: Ad infinitum. I quoted every report I could lay my
brain on concerning bisexuality and its inherent unresolved
immaturity, backing each prejudiced selection with a biased
statistic . . .

ALAN: I love when you get technical.

ARNOLD: . . . and finished her off with a quote from the man
in question himself: That if all things were equal (she and I
being the same sex), he never would have left me. Now, if that
ain't dirty logic, then what is?

ALAN (*Feigning anguish*):   Mercy! Mercy!

ARNOLD: Can that crap. This is for real.

ALAN: What're you getting so upset about? Who ever listens to you?

ARNOLD: There's always a first time. Come here and comfort me! Can't you see I'm disturbed?!?

ALAN: Why should I if you're such a rat?

ARNOLD: Because the innocent must suffer, not the guilty. This is America.

ALAN (*Laughing*):   You ain't so tough. (*Embracing*) That feel better?

ARNOLD: And she took it. Stood there staring me straight in the eye and listened to it all. Never argued, just nodded. God, you smell so good.

ALAN: Better than him?

ARNOLD: Now you're gonna start? (*Messing his hair*) He's jealous of you. Really. He told me so himself.

ALAN: Who isn't? I have you, don't I? (*Embrace*) You shouldn't have disappeared with her all afternoon. How do you think I felt?

ARNOLD: How'd you feel?

ALAN: You just shouldn't've.

ARNOLD: What're you, a baby? I gotta sit and hold your hand?

ALAN: I came up here to be with you, not him. Let's get outta here.

The lights lower as a slide appears:

CODA

Alan slips under the covers, Laurel sits in the center, the phone rings.

ARNOLD (*Answering in his sleep*):   Hello?

ED: Hi. I woke you.

ARNOLD: Good guess. Hold on a second. (*He sits up and tries to shake the sleep.*) Hello? Listen I was gonna call you later to thank you for the weekend. (*Morning cough*) As you can hear, the country air's done wonders for me.

ED: I thought I'd call to make sure you two got home all right.

ARNOLD: Yeah, fine. We drove straight through.

ED: I really enjoyed having you here. So did Laurel.

ARNOLD: I'm glad. We did too.

ED: You know, we got a lot out of having you up here. We learned a lot about our relationship.

ARNOLD: You holding seminars?

ED: Couldn't you be nice?

ARNOLD: Sorry, morning breath and all.

ED: Is Alan there with you?

ARNOLD: No, he dropped me off, then headed out to Queens to bring the car back to his mother. I guess he spent the night.

ED: Oh. But he'll be back tonight?

ARNOLD: I suppose. What's the difference?

ED: I was curious, that's all.

ARNOLD: Something wrong?

ED: Not at all.

ARNOLD: You sound funny.

ED: No. But I do have a favor to ask.

ARNOLD: Shoot.

ED: Well . . . Laurel went into the city this morning to spend a few days. Just to check on some classes. . . . Anyway, I thought

it'd be nice if you had her over to dinner or went out together for lunch or something. Just so she's not alone.

ARNOLD: Shit, look, Ed, I'm really sorry I caused trouble. . . .

ED: Oh, no. We didn't have words or anything. I just felt that it would be better if we both had time to think about our relationship.

ARNOLD: I understand.

ED: I know you do. I love her very much.

ARNOLD: Have you tried telling her that?

ED: She's not like you, Arnold. She doesn't need to be reassured every hour on the hour.

ARNOLD: An admirable quality, to be sure.

ED: Will you talk to her?

ARNOLD: Don't worry about a thing.

ED: I appreciate it.

ARNOLD: Anything else?

ED: There is one thing more.

ARNOLD: Don't stop now.

ED: Did you have a chance to correct that list yet?

ARNOLD: What list?

ED: Of the things you want. Remember, I told you to erase the check mark next to my name.

ARNOLD (*Exasperated*):   As a matter of fact, I haven't had the time. But don't you worry, I'll take care of it.

ED: Don't. I mean . . . I'd like it if you left the check mark where it is.

(*Laurel pops into the scene as Ed disappears under the covers.*)

LAUREL: So what'd you tell him?

ARNOLD: I told him I'd leave the check mark but erase the name.

LAUREL: You didn't?!?

ARNOLD: No, I didn't. But I should've. I don't know, sometimes I get the feeling he's learning, but God, it's a struggle. You going back to him?

LAUREL: I don't think so. I don't know.

ARNOLD: What'd your shrink say?

LAUREL: Not much. Nothing, as a matter of fact, nothing. He just kept asking me what I want. Over and over again, "What do you want?" "What do you want?"

ARNOLD: And what did you tell him?

LAUREL: I told him I wanted him to shut up.

ARNOLD (*Giggling*):   You didn't.

LAUREL (*Laughing too*):   No, I didn't. But I should've. What do *you* want?

ARNOLD: I wanna beer.

LAUREL: You know what I mean.

ARNOLD: What do I want? What do I want? What do I want? Well, it would have to be something witty because you're depressed and it's not enough to be funny when talking to a depressed person. One must be cleverly diverting or at least playfully bawdy. . . .

LAUREL: Your brain is hopelessly delinquent.

ARNOLD: That's what I want: A hopeless delinquent! No, I already got one of those.

LAUREL: Alan and you are wonderful together. I'm sure everything will work itself out.

ARNOLD: I didn't know there was anything that needed working out.

LAUREL: Didn't you two have words?

ARNOLD: None we haven't used before.

LAUREL: Oh. I thought that was why you returned last night instead of this morning.

ARNOLD: Not at all.

LAUREL: What happened between Alan and Ed doesn't bother you at all?

ED (*Sitting up to one side*):   You blurted it out just like that?

LAUREL (*To Ed*):   I thought he knew. I meant it as a friendly remark.

ARNOLD (*To Alan*):   With friends like her who needs newspapers?

ALAN: I tried to tell you.

ARNOLD: I must say, you picked a great time to start telling the truth.

LAUREL (*To Arnold*):   Why did you think I left?

ARNOLD (*To Laurel*):   I thought it was something I said.

LAUREL: Don't be silly.

ALAN (*To Ed*):   Are you going to tell Laurel?

ED (*To Alan*):   What I do is my own business.

LAUREL (*To Arnold*):   We respect each other's privacy.

ARNOLD: . . . and he still had energy for me. Oh, to be eighteen again! But, you and Alan didn't . . .

LAUREL: No! Why? He said we did?

ARNOLD: Well, I'm sure he meant it as a compliment . . . to both of you.

ALAN (*To Ed*):   I thought an open relationship meant that you told each other everything.

ARNOLD: You saw them together?

LAUREL: No. Ed told me about it after you left. He came into the bedroom and said he had something to discuss . . . discuss?! And he told me. He was crying. He said he was sorry. Not that he'd done it, but that he had to tell me about it. I was dumbfounded. I didn't know which of us to comfort; who was hurting more. So, I sat there. We didn't say a word, occasionally catching each other's eye and looking away again. After a while he went down to the kitchen and I packed a bag and left. I hadn't planned on leaving . . . but, it seemed the right thing to do. There I was, packed, at the door . . . so I left.

ARNOLD: That wasn't very bright.

LAUREL: And what would you have done?

ARNOLD: I'd've shoved him headfirst into a meat grinder. But I would've hung around to see what came out the other end.

LAUREL: Arnold, you don't seem to be getting the drift of this at all. He made love to someone; your lover, with me not fifty feet away. What more reason would a person possibly need to walk out on someone?

ARNOLD (*To Alan*):   I have never felt so used in my life! I wanted to put a pillow over her face and snuff her out. (*Mocking*) "I hadn't planned on leaving." The gall! "What more reason would a person possibly need to walk out?" The nerve!!

LAUREL: So, this is the Nursery. It's not at all what I'd expected from Ed's description. I like it though. It's got a coziness . . . a warmth. I can feel it.

ARNOLD (*To Laurel*):   Thanks.

LAUREL: If this is the Nursery, does that make you the Nurse?

ARNOLD: Registered with the A.M.A. You need one? (*Laurel nods and begins to cry*) Nurse Arnold to the rescue. (*He takes her*

in his arms like a baby.) I accept Blue Cross, Blue Shield, and Blue Nun. Hurts, huh?

LAUREL: Like a claw in my stomach. Just once in my life I'd like to have an affair go on the rocks after the passion wears off; when I'm bored with the routine, the sex, the talk. I'd love to know what it feels like to have the flame rekindled by jealousy instead of this . . . having the rug pulled out from under me like this. Just once I'd like to be standing on sure ground when the blow hits instead of crawling around on my hands and knees like a baby.

ARNOLD: You want a hell of a lot out of life. Don'tcha? I'd settle for being able to say to someone, "I love you," and, whether I meant it or not, finding them still in bed the next morning.

ALAN: All you had to do was ask me.

ARNOLD: Ask you what?

ALAN: Not to fool around with anyone else, and I wouldn't have.

LAUREL: But you never asked me.

ED: Because I wanted you to feel that you could.

ALAN: You mean, you wanted me to feel that *you* could. All those nights you spent out in them backrooms: How do you think I felt?

ARNOLD: That's not the same thing at all. I didn't even know those people's names.

ALAN: That makes a difference?

LAUREL: You mean, you want me to see other men?

ARNOLD: No. But I want you to feel free to.

ALAN: I do. And I did. So, what are you so upset about?

ED: It's the kind of relationship you said you wanted.

LAUREL: Just because I said that's what I want doesn't mean

that's what I want. I mean, that's what I want but that doesn't mean that I'm necessarily ready for it.

ALAN: You're being ridiculous.

ARNOLD: You telling me that you don't see any difference between my innocent jaunts to the backroom and your vile debauchery this weekend?

ALAN: Not really.

ARNOLD: Well. There you have it!

ALAN: There I have what?

ARNOLD: Don't be such a smart-ass!

LAUREL (*To Arnold*): It's my own fault for expecting something different. The only thing different about each of the affairs in my life is the way they dumped me. Not even the way so much as the words.

ARNOLD: I know what you mean. My favorite kiss-offs are those little speeches: "I really dig you, baby. You're the kind that I could really fall for. But, I'm not ready to fall, so *Adiós.*"

LAUREL: I much prefer the Continental version: "We've got a good thing going; let's not mess it up by getting too involved."

ARNOLD: How about, "Let's not make any promises we'll regret later?"

LAUREL: You ever hear the one about the trial separation?

ARNOLD: As often as I've heard about their reconciliation.

LAUREL: "I've got to try my wings."

ARNOLD: "I've got to repark the car."

LAUREL: "I've got to live free!"

ARNOLD: "She meant nothing to me!" Oops. Sorry.

LAUREL: That's all right. It's nothing I haven't heard before.

ARNOLD: Gee, but it's GREAT to have someone else to blame. (*They both laugh.*)

LAUREL: I don't understand; how could Ed ever have let you get away?

ARNOLD: I'm lousy in bed. It's true. I don't relax enough. I guess I'm just an old-fashioned kind of guy: I hardly ever enjoy sex with someone I know. So, you ready to call home?

LAUREL: I don't know. What do you think?

ARNOLD: I think I'm the wrong person to ask.

ALAN (*Coupling with Arnold*):   That's the first thing you've said all week that's made sense.

ARNOLD: Look who's talking.

LAUREL (*Coupling with Ed*):   I should at least give him a chance to explain.

ALAN: She'll stay with him. They were made for each other.

LAUREL: I owe him as much.

ARNOLD: It's wrong.

LAUREL: After all, what have I got to lose.

ARNOLD: It's all wrong.

LAUREL: Otherwise . . . what was it all for?

ARNOLD: I can't tell you how strongly I feel that it's wrong! (*They are alone in the light.*) You were wrong to do what you did! . . . Though I know why you did. And Ed was wrong to do what he did! . . . Though I know why he did. And Laurel was wrong to use what you two did!! . . . Though I know why she did. And I was wrong to do everything I did! . . . But I did. I don't know, maybe it all evens out in the end. I mean, if two wrongs don't make a right . . . maybe four do.

ALAN: So the score's all evened up.

ARNOLD: I can't tell with these "Make-'em-up-as-you-go-along" rules. Monogamy's a much easier system to keep track of.

ALAN: Well, look at it this way: Ed's got what he wants—a warm body in bed with a very attractive break in his routine. And Laurel's got what she wants—Ed in bed. . . .

ARNOLD: With a million new fascinating problems to discuss with her shrink.

ALAN: And we've got what we want . . . each other.

ARNOLD: You're awful pushy for a kid who ain't old enough to pee straight.

ALAN (*Lying back*):   Come here and I'll show you how pushy.

ARNOLD (*Delighted*):   Just let me turn out the lights.

ALAN: Why do you wanna turn out the lights?

ARNOLD: Because, even in times like these one must retain a degree of the old cherished decorum.

ALAN: Well, aren't we civilized.

ARNOLD: Terribly!

ALAN: Wait. There's one more thing I'd like to ask you.

ARNOLD (*Into his arms*):   The answer is yes.

ALAN: But you don't know the question.

ARNOLD: Doesn't matter. I'm too tired to argue about anything so whatever it is, the answer is yes.

ALAN: Good. Because I love you too.

ARNOLD (*Pulling away*):   Oh, for God's sake, Alan, after everything we've been through this weekend . . .

ALAN: Oh, shut up! (*Embarrassed*) Can't you take a joke?

The music begins to play as Arnold sits up, staring straight ahead in bewildered shock. As the bed begins to leave the stage he lies back into Alan's arms in hopeless surrender. Alan feeds him a piece of cake as the bed disappears offstage.

A slide:

EPILOGUE

The quartet music is joined by a piano. Upstage we see the small ornate stage and baby grand piano of a nightclub. The pianist is playing the introduction to a violent, angry love song. Arnold enters in rehearsal clothes, carrying his music and sings the song. His is a passionate interpretation. The song ends.

ARNOLD (*To pianist. Making a note on the score.*):   That oughta fog up their glasses and empty their mugs. We'll use it between "Cry Me a River" and "Who's Sorry Now?" Just as a change of pace.

LAUREL (*She's been watching from the wings.*):   God, you're depressing.

ARNOLD: Laurel? Oh, no!

LAUREL: Thanks a lot.

ARNOLD: No, I didn't mean: Oh, no: not you. I meant: Oh, no: you two had another fight.

LAUREL: Oh, no: not at all.

ARNOLD: Really?

LAUREL: You say that like you don't believe it.

ARNOLD: Oh, no.

LAUREL: Let's not start that again. Aren't you going to say hello?

ARNOLD: Hello. Sorry, but this just ain't my day. My maid called in sick, my cleaning came in late, we've got these new numbers to rehearse . . .

LAUREL: Maybe I'd better not bother you.

ARNOLD: No, stay. I could use a little gossip in the midst of all this reality. (*To pianist*) Five minutes, hon. (*Taking a chair off a little table*) Here, make yourself at home.

LAUREL: Oh, the man in front asked me to give you this. (*She hands him a small parcel.*)

ARNOLD (*Taking down a chair for himself*):   Thanks. Here, sit down.

LAUREL: You really like that?

ARNOLD (*Opening the package*):   What?

LAUREL: Songs about suicide, lost love, growing old disgracefully.

ARNOLD: Pays the rent.

LAUREL: Funny, but I always imagined you'd sing comic songs. Y'know, novelty numbers.

ARNOLD: I'm strictly Torch. While all the other kids were listening to the Beatles, Sam the Sham, and the Dave Clark Five, I was home lip-synching Billie Holiday, Jane Froman, and Helen Morgan. As I got older I switched to *Lucia di Lammermoor, Tosca,* and *Manon.* But it was always tragic stuff. Something about taking all that misery and making it into something. . . . Anyway, the audiences like it. I guess getting hurt is one thing we all have in common.

LAUREL: You sound like one of your songs.

ARNOLD: I *am* one of my songs. (*Taking out a leash and collar from the package*) Oh, look, it's my wedding present to Alan.

LAUREL: And you told me you weren't into that stuff.

ARNOLD: It's for Alan's dog.

LAUREL: I didn't know he had a dog.

ARNOLD: He doesn't. But he will tomorrow when I give him one.

LAUREL: You got him a dog? What kind?

ARNOLD: Well, y'know they say that a dog grows to look like its master, or that a master grows to look like his dog . . . so, I got him a big, fat, home-loving Saint Bernard. It should be quite a battle.

LAUREL: Perfect. So, you two are getting married?

ARNOLD: As married as two men can illegally get. Actually it's more of a contract-signing party. After that weekend the four of us spent together we decided to draw up a few rules and regulations, just so we'd know where we stood with each other. Well, we've spent our every waking, nonworking hour on this document and we're finally ready to sign it. (*Holds up a rolled-up piece of parchment*)

LAUREL: That's wonderful. May I see it? (*She opens it.*) It's one sentence long.

ARNOLD: Well, we had a little trouble agreeing on some issues. This is sort of a basic working philosophy which we can amend and elaborate on as we feel necessary.

LAUREL (*Reading*):   "We, Arnold and Alan, being of sound mind and social-diseaseless bodies, hereby swear to take equal responsibility for walking and feeding the dog."

ARNOLD (*Taking it away*):   Like I said, it's just a basis. Anyway, the ceremony's tomorrow after the show and we'd love for you to come.

LAUREL: I wish we'd known. But we've already made plans to take care of a few important things. Which brings me to my reason for coming to see you.

ARNOLD: . . . always a reason.

LAUREL: You know, now that it's time I don't know how to say it.

ARNOLD: Sounds serious.

LAUREL: It is.

ARNOLD: Be blunt.

LAUREL: Ed and I are engaged to be married.

ARNOLD (*Blank*):   Oh.

LAUREL: You and Alan, Ed and me. Kind of ironic, huh?

ARNOLD: That's the word for it. Well, congratulations. I'm sure you two will be very happy together.

LAUREL: Thank you.

ARNOLD: When was all this decided?

LAUREL: I guess about the same time you were drawing up your contract. We talked a lot when I went back to the farm; about what we wanted out of a relationship, what we wanted from each other . . . and we figured after that weekend . . . well, if we could get through a thing like that and still be together, then we could get through anything. Even marriage.

ARNOLD: I could hardly say I didn't expect it, but I could hardly say I did expect it. . . . What I could say is that I'm happy for you. Hey, I'm gonna call Ed right now. . . .

LAUREL: I'd rather you didn't. Ed doesn't know I'm here. As a matter of fact, he's planning on coming by tonight to tell you himself. And I'd like to ask you not to mention my visit. After all, he did want to tell you first.

ARNOLD: Then why did you tell me?

LAUREL: I don't know. That's not true. I was scared that you'd say something negative. Make fun of him or try to talk him out of it. Arnold, everything's going so well between us, but Ed is still shaky. And the wrong word from you . . .

ARNOLD: That's ridiculous.

LAUREL: No, it's realistic.

ARNOLD: You're just being silly. Really you are. The two of you will get married and live happily ever after and I'm very happy

for you. And just to prove it . . . I'll be a bridesmaid at the wedding. So, what color are we wearing?

LAUREL: Oh, it would mean so much to both of us to have you there, but the wedding is at my parents' home in Massachusetts and . . . it's really going to be small . . . so we're limiting the guests to just immediate family.

ARNOLD: That's all right; I look terrible in green.

LAUREL: I'm sorry, really. Well, I'd better let you get back to your rehearsal. I've kept you long enough. It was wonderful seeing you again. And as soon as we get set up we'll have you over for dinner or something.

ARNOLD: Sure. We'd love that.

LAUREL: You won't say anything to Ed?

ARNOLD: My wrists are sealed.

LAUREL: Pardon?

ARNOLD: An old fag joke.

LAUREL: Well, bye-bye. Give my best to Alan. (*Laurel exits and Arnold returns to piano.*)

ARNOLD: Hey, Max, you know "The Wedding March"? Never mind. Let's try the closing number.

(*The pianist begins to play as Arnold climbs up onto the piano.*)
It's over, concluded, expired, that's it.
I've had it, been through it, my limit's been hit.
It's not that I doubt your love for me,
Your passion or sincerity,
Your faith, hope, trust, or charity,
What I doubt . . . is you.
You cheated, you lied, dear. You two-timed me twice.
And that makes four times, dear. And that isn't nice.
And now you've the nerve to say to me,
Your wife likes being one of three.

So I'll genteelly answer thee:
Go blow it out your shoe.
I can't live on love alone.
Want somebody all my own.
I can't live on love alone.
You can argue but it's true,
Three can't live as cheap as two.
I can't live on love alone.
Fidelity is out of fashion,
Variety is everybody's passion.
Drugs can keep you copulating till you cash in.
And when you're through they'll bury you with your wife.
One-night stands are not my quarry,
I signed up for repertory.
No, I won't live on love alone.
Keep my number by the phone
Call me if you should atone.
But I can't live, no I can't live . . . on love alone.
(The lights fade to black.)

THE END

WIDOWS AND CHILDREN FIRST!

WIDOWS AND CHILDREN FIRST! *premiered at La Mama E.T.C. on October 25, 1979, with the following cast:*

ARNOLD BECKOFF	Harvey Fierstein
DAVID	Frederick Allen
ED	Will Jeffries
MRS. BECKOFF	Estelle Getty

Directed by Eric Concklin
Stage Design by Bill Stabile
Lighting by Cheryl Thacker
Costumes by Carla Lawrence
Production Stage Manager: Richard Jakiel

CHARACTERS

ED REISS: Now forty, still handsome, still with a disarming boyish charm and innocence.

DAVID: Fifteen going on thirty. A wonderfully bright and handsome boy.

ARNOLD: Thirty, as witty and personable as ever.

MRS. BECKOFF: Arnold's mother. Sixtyish. A real Jewish mother. A fighter.

TIME

Five years after the action of FUGUE IN A NURSERY.

SYNOPSIS OF SCENES

1) Arnold's apartment, 7 A.M. on a Thursday in June.
2) Same, 5 P.M. that day.
3) A bench in the park below, immediately following.
4) The apartment, 6 A.M. the next morning.

> AUTHOR'S NOTE:
> PACE!!!!!!! And honesty!

SCENE ONE

The stage is a realistically represented living/dining room and kitchenette. There is an entrance door, a bathroom door, and a hallway that leads to two offstage bedrooms. It is the set of a conventional sit-com with a convertible sofa, windows overlooking Central Park, and assorted objects and props. There is also a miniset for Scene 3, which is described herein. As the lights come up, a radio is blaring Fanny Brice singing "I'm Cooking Breakfast for the One I Love." Ed is busily cooking. The song ends. . . .

RADIO: It's seven-eighteen in the Big Apple and this is Hi Tide wishin' you a good, good Mornin'. (*A chorus of singers twitter,* "Good Morning, Good Morning, Good Morning to you!") And now for all you sleepyheads what just can't shake them night-time blues, number one on our hot-pick chart and guaranteed to raise the dead . . . Edward O. Wilson's "I Was Born This Way, What's Your Excuse." (*Music begins.*)

ED (*Quickly changing to a mellower station*): There's a thought to start the day.

DAVID (*From within the bathroom*): Arnold? You got anything I could put on my eye?

ED (*Calling back*): He's in the bedroom.

DAVID: What?

ED: Arnold's still in the bedroom.

DAVID: Never mind, I found somethin'.

ED (*Hollering down the hall*): Arnold, you up? Breakfast is on the table.

DAVID: What?

ED: I was talking to Arnold. (*An explosion in the kitchen*)

ARNOLD (*Offstage*): What the hell was that?

ED (*Running to kitchen*):   I think the coffee's ready.

ARNOLD (*Enters in bathrobe and bunny-shaped slippers*):   And a "Good Morning, Good Morning, Good Morning to you." You're making breakfast? Aren't you an angel. Smells terrible.

ED: My specialty: Eggs, onions, and kippered herring en casserole.

ARNOLD: Toast for me, I'm on a diet.

ED: Since when?

ARNOLD: Since I heard the specialty. (*Yelling down hall*) David, you up yet?

ED: He's in the throne room.

ARNOLD (*Knocks on door*):   Hurry up, Sugar-Puss, you'll be late for school.

ED: You look well-rested.

ARNOLD: I feel like freeze-dried death. (*Sees mess*) Ed, since when do you make coffee in a pressure cooker?

ED: The water boils faster.

DAVID (*Through crack in door*):   Everybody ready? Stand back from the door and hang onto your apron strings 'cause here I come. (*Enters modeling a three-piece suit*) Well? Whatcha think?

ARNOLD (*As Ed whistles approval*):   What's the occasion? Ms. Schnable isn't due till next week.

DAVID: But your mother is due today. Think she'll like me?

ARNOLD: Who'd dare not like my baby?

DAVID: And look, I put some gook on. You can't even see the black eye.

ARNOLD (*Examining*):   When I think of that kid hitting you, I wanna tear down to that school and beat the shit outta him.

ED (*Serving the food*):   Your maternal instincts are incredible.

DAVID: I can take care of myself.

ARNOLD: I see.

DAVID: Would you stop.

ED: What'd the two of you fight about anyway?

DAVID: He called me something I didn't like, so I slugged him. (*Helping Arnold fold the couch*)

ED: So how'd you end up with the black eye?

DAVID: I didn't slug him fast enough.

ARNOLD: That's my son, The Champ.

DAVID (*Posing*):   That's me, Champ David.

ED: What was it he called you?

DAVID: A douche bag.

ARNOLD: How fifties.

ED: Soup's on!

ARNOLD (*Exiting to bathroom*):   You stay away from that kid today. I ain't got no money to buy no new suit.

DAVID: He's somethin', ain't he? What's with this dentist music? (*Switches to rock station. It is the same song only discoed.*) Much better.

ED (*Holding out chair*):   May I seat you, sir?

DAVID: Don't mind if you do. (*Sits*) What died in here?

ED: Breakfast. (*Holding plate over David's head*) I cooked it myself. Any complaints?

DAVID: From me? Are you kidding? You know me, always ready for a gastronomic adventure. (*Ed sets down plate.*) Looks wonderful. Could you pass the salt? How'd you sleep?

ED: The couch and I aren't speaking.

DAVID: It's only your fourth night. You'll get used to it. Could

you pass the pepper? I slept on it for weeks while we worked on my room, and I'm still walking.

ED: I'll probably be able to find a place by the weekend.

DAVID: What's your rush? Can I have the ketchup? It's great having you here. Could you pass the mustard?

ED: Something wrong with the food?

DAVID: Not at all. Very tasty. Can I have the mayo, please? (*Ed shoots a look.*) Hold the mayo. (*Tastes it*) Mmmmmm. Delicious. Oh, I forgot, your wife called.

ED: When?

DAVID: Middle of the night. I tried to wake you but you were out of it. I told her you'd call back in the morning.

ED: What time did she call?

DAVID: Musta been around two. Somethin' about some papers for you to sign.

ED: Thanks. I'd better call. Help yourself to seconds, there's plenty.

DAVID: And I was worried. (*Ed goes to phone.*) You sure are a heavy sleeper. The phone rang five times.

ED: What were you doing up so late?

DAVID: Answering the phone.

ED (*Into phone*): Hello, Laurel? What's up? . . . Couldn't that have waited till morning? . . . I don't think it's fair to wake the whole house. . . .

ARNOLD (*Entering*): Hey, Champ, remember to bring back your report card. I signed it.

DAVID: Where'd you put it?

ARNOLD: By the door.

DAVID: Is Ms. Schnable really coming next week?

ARNOLD: Every third Thursday for the next three months. So stay outta trouble and pray that eye heals. I wish this damned probation period was over already. Gives me the creeps havin' someone check up on us all the time.

DAVID: What's the rush? When the adoption papers come through we stop gettin' the foster-care checks and we need the money.

ARNOLD: You may find this hard to believe, but I didn't take you in for the money.

DAVID: Then you're the first.

ARNOLD (*Seeing Ed*):   Who's on the phone?

DAVID: Ed.

ARNOLD: I thought I recognized the voice.

ED: . . . Laurel, I wish you wouldn't. . . . Not on the phone!

ARNOLD: There's nothing more frustrating than a one-sided conversation.

DAVID: There's another kind?

ED: . . . I really don't want to discuss this now. . . . Because, there are other people in the room.

DAVID: Don't mind us. (*Arnold swats him.*)

ED: . . . Can we please talk about this later? . . . Hello? . . . Laurel, are you there? . . . For God's sake, are you crying?

ARNOLD (*Under his breath*):   Animal.

ED: Laurel, please. I'll come over and we can talk. . . . I don't know when. This afternoon. I don't know. . . . All right, I'll see you then. . . . Bye-bye. (*Hangs up*)

DAVID: She gave you a hard time, huh? (*Arnold swats him again.*) Ow! That hurt.

ARNOLD (*Big smile*):   Want some coffee?

ED: No, I'm fine. After four days of those calls I think I'm getting used to them. I mean, I understand why she calls; she's confused, alone . . . What I can't understand is her damned crying.

ARNOLD: Of course it's just a wild guess, but do you suppose it's because she's confused and alone?

ED: Well, I don't see why. This separation wasn't all my idea.

ARNOLD: Look, Ed, I realize this is a trying time for you and I'll gladly supply a place to sleep, a home-thrown meal, and all the amoral support I can muster, but you've got to keep the gory details to yourself.

ED (*Grandly*):   Ah, what price compassion?!!

ARNOLD: Fifty bucks an hour and I don't take credit cards.

ED: Fifty?

ARNOLD: Hey, talk's cheap, but listening'll cost ya. Buck up, Bronco, things are bound to get easier.

ED: Oh, I know. I just wish she wouldn't carry on like that. You wouldn't believe the crazy accusations she was making. . . .

ARNOLD: Ed, I'm serious. I really don't want to hear about it.

ED (*Mock pout*):   Some friend you are.

ARNOLD: I'm your ex-lover, Ed, not your friend.

DAVID: Oooooh. The heavy stuff. And it ain't even eight o'clock.

ARNOLD (*Turning David's head back to his plate*):   Don't talk with your mouth full.

DAVID: But my mouth's . . . (*Arnold glares.*) Is full. Very full.

ARNOLD: I didn't say that to be mean. Really. But I can't help remembering a phone call not unlike that one from someone in this very room, if you get my drift.

ED: Didn't think of that.

ARNOLD: Well, do. Please do. And please don't ask for any advice, 'cause you don't want to hear what I have to say.

DAVID: Heartbreaker. (*Arnold glares.*) I'm eating. I'm eating.

ARNOLD: All this and my mother too.

ED: Well, I'll see Laurel this afternoon and hopefully end these midnight calls.

ARNOLD: That would be lovely. And while you're there could you see if she'd mind letting you stay with her Wednesday night? The Department of Child Welfare will be arriving early in the person of Our Ms. Schnable and I've got enough to explain without you on the couch.

ED: I'm good enough for your mother but not for David's social worker?

ARNOLD: It has nothing to do with being good enough. Ms. Schnable frowns on casual cohabitation.

ED: Casual? We've known each other for six years.

ARNOLD: Four of which you spent married to another woman. (*To David*) Take a glass of milk.

ED (*Pouring David's milk*):   I get it, it's not me she'll object to but my bisexuality.

ARNOLD: Could we please leave your perverted preferences un-purported this joyous morn?

ED: Bigot!

ARNOLD: Reactionary Chickenshit!

DAVID: Please, not in front of the child.

ED: I could lie and tell her I'm gay.

ARNOLD: Come on.

ED: Don't you think I could make a convincing homosexual?

DAVID: You could make this convincing homosexual.

ARNOLD: David! Besides, if she thought you were gay, she'd never believe you slept on the couch.

ED: I could show you the scars.

ARNOLD: I could show you the door.

DAVID: I could show you a good time.

ED and ARNOLD: David!!

DAVID: Well, I'd love to sit and chat with you grown-up types, but we straight-C students pride ourselves on our punk-tuality.

ARNOLD: Go brush your teeth.

DAVID: Oh, Maaaaaaaa!

ARNOLD: Don't you "Oh, Ma" me. March. And don't call me Ma in front of my mother. (*David exits. Ed giggles.*) Having a good time?

ED: Sorry, but you do act like his mother.

ARNOLD: Guess I do. But this parent act's still new to me. I can't quite get the hang of being mother, father, friend, and con- fessor all rolled into one.

ED: You're doin' great.

ARNOLD: Think so?

ED: You're the best mother-father-friend-confessor I've ever seen. You've just got to let go a little more.

ARNOLD: I will. Geez, I can't wait for my mother to get here; I can mother-smother David, she can mother-smother me . . .

ED: And I can mother-smother referee.

ARNOLD: Laugh now, Leroy, but we're gonna need one. Y'know, this stuff smells awful, but it tastes much worse.

ED: Be nice or I'll tell people it's your recipe.

ARNOLD: You don't have to threaten me twice.

ED: I'm enjoying being here with you and David enormously. I want you to know that.

ARNOLD: Good.

ED: You ever wonder what things would be like if I'd never met Laurel?

ARNOLD: That all depends, did I meet Alan?

ED: Of course not. If I didn't meet Laurel you wouldn't have met Alan.

ARNOLD: Oh. So that's how it works. Well, did I adopt David?

ED: That's what I'm asking. Would we have stayed together and would we have adopted David?

ARNOLD: How should I know?

ED: Well, didn't you ever wonder?

ARNOLD: Ed, I have enough trouble with the "What nows" without starting in on the "What ifs."

ED: Yeah, but haven't you ever thought about what things would be like if we'd stayed together?

ARNOLD: I guess so. When Alan died I thought about a lot of crazy things. I'm sure you were among them.

ED: And?

ARNOLD: I don't know. Why, what do you think?

ED: I think we might've been very happy together. It's possible.

ARNOLD: It's also possible that it could be me you just walked out on.

ED: I didn't just walk out. And who just said they didn't want to discuss this?

ARNOLD: Who's discussing? I'm simply pointing out a certain pattern a certain person seems to have fallen into.

ED: People do make mistakes.

ARNOLD: I wanna write that down.

ED: . . . and sometimes they are even forgiven for them.

ARNOLD: Oh, don't be so melodramatic. I forgave you years ago. I don't think I could've been happy with Alan if I hadn't.

ED: Maybe you and your mother should spend some time alone. I can still find a hotel.

ARNOLD: You're staying here and that's an order. You wouldn't leave me unprotected at a time like this, would you? Of course you would. But you ain't gonna. My mother isn't going to feature the idea of my becoming a father, and your professional opinion as an American educator will prove invaluable.

ED: She'll say I'm prejudiced.

ARNOLD: She'll say a lot of things. You'll learn not to listen. More coffee?

ED (*Hands his cup*):   Please.

ARNOLD: (*Making coffee and cleaning up*) My mother's all right. Basically. When I was a kid we had a healthy Mother/Son relationship. A delicate blend of love, concern, and guilt. We never talked much but when we did we kept things on an honest level. I mean, I told her I was gay when I was thirteen.

ED: You knew when you were thirteen?

ARNOLD: When I was thirteen I knew everything. Senility set in sometime after. And look at me now: On the threshold of thirty I need a calculator to write a check, a cookbook to fry an egg, and Dial-a-Prayer to do the rest. (*To David*) Hurry up in there, you'll be late.

DAVID (*Offstage*):   Don't rush an artist.

ARNOLD: What was I saying?

ED: Something about your mother.

ARNOLD: My mother: the Rita Hayworth of Brighton Beach. We always kept an open line of communication, that is, until

my father died; then, I don't know, something happened, she clammed up. I mean, we saw each other more than ever, and we spoke daily on the phone, but somehow we managed to say less than ever. It became a contest to see who could talk most but say least.

ED: It's called Adult Conversation.

ARNOLD: Thank you, Tom Snyder. Where was I?

ED: Your mother.

ARNOLD: My mother: the Sylvia Sydney of Bay Twenty-fifth Street. I think the root of it was my father's death. She refused to talk about it, or about how she was coping alone. But Alan and I were living together then, so I always had a source of subject matter in him.

ED: She knew Alan?

ARNOLD: Oh, yeah. And they got along as long as I didn't call him my lover. She preferred to call him my "Friend." Anyway, she retired, moved to Florida, which reduced our relationship to weekly phone calls and biannual visitations. And then Alan died and I was expected to observe the same vow of silence about him as she had about my father. So we've learned to make meaningful conversation from the weather, general health, and my brother's marital status. I never even told her how Alan was killed. She assumed it was a car accident and I didn't bother correcting her.

ED: So now you don't know how to tell her about David.

ARNOLD: Oh, she knows about David. But she assumed he was my roommate and I . . .

ED: . . . you didn't bother correcting her.

ARNOLD: It's not the telling that frightens me. But I shake when I think of the long-muzzled floodgates of motherly advice that will unleash when she gets wind of this.

ED: How bad could it possibly be?

ARNOLD: Stick around, kid.

DAVID (*Entering*):   How's these? (*Big smile*) And look, I'm taking the brush with me so's I can give them a swipe before my big entrance. Think Granny'll be impressed?

ARNOLD: David, you can put your elbows on the table, use vile and abusive language, even pass gas loudly during conversation. But whatever you do . . . don't call her Granny!

DAVID: You could save yourself a load of grief if you'd just let me break the good news to her.

ARNOLD: Thanks, but I've heard your subtle mouth at work.

DAVID: Don't say I didn't offer. (*Phone rings*) I'll get it.

ED (*To Arnold*):   You want tea?

ARNOLD: Why not?

DAVID (*Into phone*):   Sister Arnold's House of Hope. You pay, we pray. Brother David speaking.

ARNOLD (*Grabs phone*):   Give me that. Hello? . . . Oh, hi, Murray. . . . No, that was David's idea of discretion.

DAVID: Think I have a future in the Diplomatic Corps?

ARNOLD: Hang on a sec. (*To David*) Don't you ever answer the phone like that again. What if this was Ms. Schnable? Have you got a comb? (*He produces one.*) A handkerchief? (*He moans.*) March!

ED (*Handing tea to Arnold as David reads report card*):   A handkerchief? Really, Arnold.

DAVID: What the hell is this? (*Reads from card*) "I'm proud of his improvement and am sure he'll do even better on his finals."

ARNOLD: It said "Parent's Comments" and I had to write something.

DAVID: No you didn't. (*Storms to bedroom*)

ARNOLD: Murray, can I call you back after I get my little men off to work? Okay, I'll call . . . David! Hang up that extension! . . . No, you can't have a divorce. We're not married. . . . Murray? I'll call you back. (*Hangs up*) All right, what'd I do wrong now?

ED: The kids like to brag that they forged their parents' signatures. But if there's a sensible comment like that then everyone will know it's the real thing.

ARNOLD: How was I supposed to know? God, he makes me feel old.

ED: Don't worry about it. What time is the Great Arrival?

ARNOLD: I don't know. I figure around noon.

DAVID (*Enters with hankie*): I'm gettin' outta here before you think of something else.

ARNOLD: Where are your schoolbooks?

DAVID: In school.

ARNOLD: How'd you do your homework?

DAVID: Astral projection.

ARNOLD: You forgetting something?

DAVID: What now?

ARNOLD: Don't I get a kiss good-bye?

DAVID (*Laughs*): You're unreal. (*Warm hug and kiss*) I love you.

ARNOLD: Me too. Now, get outta here. You're late.

DAVID (*Exiting*): Have a nice day, Ed. You too . . . Ma. (*Out*)

ED: Men kissing. What's this world coming to?

ARNOLD: My father and brother and I all kissed. It's called affection. Aren't you going to work?

ED: It's Brooklyn Day. My school's closed.

ARNOLD: Only the Brooklyn schools?

ED: And Queens.

ARNOLD: Queens too? Sounds like Affirmative Action at work. (*Sees Ed clearing dishes*) That's all right. I'll do them.

ED: Then I'll go for the papers. Maybe I'll get a lead on an apartment.

ARNOLD: Hurry back. I ain't facin' her alone. Do you and your mother get along?

ED: Sure. No problem. That is, as long as I remember to call her every now and then. And send her a card on her Birthday. And Mother's Day. And Christmas. Oh, and of course there's Valentine's Day, and St. Patrick's Day, Labor Day, Thanksgiving, Easter, Fourth of July, Election Day, and Christopher Columbus's Birthday.

ARNOLD: You forgot Halloween.

ED: That's her Anniversary.

ARNOLD: How romantic.

ED: Where's my blue jacket?

ARNOLD: My room, left side. (*Ed exits.*) Ed? You ever tell your folks you were gay?

ED (*Reentering*):   But I'm not.

ARNOLD: All right, bisexual. Don't be so technical. I ain't Kinsey.

ED: No.

ARNOLD: Never?

ED: You need anything from the store?

ARNOLD: Wait a minute. I mean, I know you were in the closet when we were together, but I figured once you got married you'd feel secure enough to tell them.

ED: Once I got married there was nothing to tell them. (*Defensive*) And I wasn't in the closet.

ARNOLD: Ed, when the only people who know you're gay are the ones you're gaying with, that's called in the closet.

ED: Arnold, you may enjoy broadcasting your sexual preferences but I happen to believe that who I sleep with is my business and not the world's.

ARNOLD: We'll discuss the world later, I'm asking about your mother.

ED: Why put them through that?

ARNOLD: Through what?

ED: Making them feel that in some way they failed me or did something wrong. You know the trip.

ARNOLD: But you could explain to them that they had nothing to do with it. Well, not that way, anyway.

ED: They'd still be miserable. Besides, I really don't think it's any of their business.

ARNOLD: You told them about Laurel, didn't you?

ED: We were married.

ARNOLD: You lived together for a year first. You sayin' they didn't know about her till after the wedding?

ED: Arnold, you told your parents, they accepted it, and I'm very happy for all of you. All right? Jesus. Your mother flies in for a visit and I get a Gay Consciousness-Raising lecture.

ARNOLD: You have a Prim-Evil attitude about your sexuality, Mr. Reiss.

ED: Enough?

ARNOLD: And they wonder why we broke up.

ED: Arnold, you have nothing to worry about. Believe me, your

mother will see you and David together and will be pleased with both of you.

ARNOLD: You really think I'm doing good with him?

ED: You've taken a punk kid who's spent the last three years on the streets and in juvenile court and turned him into a home-living, fun-loving, school-going teenager in all of six months. Yes, I think you're doing good with him.

ARNOLD: I wish Alan was here. He woulda been great with the kid.

ED: I'll see you later.

ARNOLD: Don't be too long.

ED (*Exiting*):   Give me an hour.

ARNOLD: See ya. (*Runs to door*) Ed? We need milk! Skimmed!! (*The phone rings. Arnold grunts and answers.*)

ARNOLD: Hello? . . . Oh, hi, Murray. . . . Not much. The usual assortment of early-morning crises. What's up by you?

ED (*Tears back into the room*):   Arnold, she's here!

ARNOLD: Hang on, Murr. (*To Ed*) What?

ED: She's here. She's headed up the stairs.

ARNOLD: Can't be. It's too early.

ED: There's a woman on the stairs checking all the apartment numbers.

ARNOLD: What'd she look like?

ED (*Indicating*):   This tall, this wide, carrying a suitcase and a shopping bag.

ARNOLD: Mayday, Murray! I'll call you back.

ED: Calm down, Arnold. (*As Arnold runs around the room*)

ARNOLD: She can't see the place looking like this. She'll walk through the door and head straight for the vacuum cleaner.

MA (*In the open doorway*):   Well, I might change my shoes first.

ARNOLD: Ma. Hi. Come on in.

MA (*Friendly to Ed*):   Hello. You must be David.

ED: No, I'm Ed.

MA (*Taking back her extended hand*):   How do you do. I'm the mother.

ARNOLD (*Taking her bags*):   I really didn't expect you this early.

MA: Obviously.

ED (*Backing out*):   Well, I've got to be off. Lovely meeting you, Mrs. Beckoff. I'll remember the milk. (*Out. Then back in.*) Skimmed. (*Out*)

MA: Nice-looking boy. Who is he?

ARNOLD: That's Ed. . . .

MA: That's enough—for now I'm sorry I snapped at him but that bus ride from the airport. . . . I had to stand the whole way. There wasn't a man on that bus would give me his seat. I'm telling you, Arnold, Women's Liberation is giving me varicose veins. So, let me look at you. How do you feel. You look good.

ARNOLD: Good compared to the last time you saw me.

MA: The last time I saw you was at your friend's funeral. You're supposed to look lousy at funerals; it shows respect. You could stand a shave.

ARNOLD: I just got up. Coffee?

MA: A glass of tea. And a can of Lysol. What's that stench?

ARNOLD: Ed cooked breakfast.

MA: So I know he's not the cook. Pretty wallpaper.

ARNOLD: It's not wallpaper. I stenciled the design.

MA: Next time use wallpaper. Covers a multitude of sins. Looks

nice enough, but why you'd give up that lovely place in Brooklyn to move to Manhattan, God only knows.

ARNOLD: The other place had one bedroom. We needed two.

MA: I thought your roommate's name was David.

ARNOLD: It is. He isn't here right now.

MA: Three men, two bedrooms . . . I'll have my tea first.

ARNOLD: Ed's transitory. The sofa's a convertible. Honey?

MA: Lemon. I brought my own Sweet 'n Low . . . from the plane. You don't get much light here.

ARNOLD: We get what you call "indirect semishade." It's good for the plants.

MA: So's manure. Looks comfortable. How do you find the roaches?

ARNOLD: I turn on the lights. (*A little laugh at his little joke*)

MA: Arnold, when a man's with his friends he makes wife jokes. When he's with his wife he makes mother jokes. And when he's with his mother . . . he lets her make the jokes. (*Arnold gets the message.*) You speak to your brother?

ARNOLD: He was over for dinner last week.

MA: He brought a girl?

ARNOLD: Andrea.

MA: He's still seeing her? Any talk of marriage?

ARNOLD: You'll see him tomorrow, you can ask yourself.

MA: And be accused of meddling? Bite your tongue.

ARNOLD (*Entering with tea tray, Ma is seated on sofa*): Are you getting shorter?

MA: No, I'm sitting down. So, who's this Ed?

ARNOLD: A friend. Tell me about Florida. Anyone special in your life?

MA: Not particularly. You mean Ed's a friend-friend or a euphemism-friend?

ARNOLD: He used to be a euphemism, now he's just a friend. Why aren't you seeing anyone?

MA: Because the only ones who ask me out are old men and the one thing I don't need is to become a nursemaid for some *alter kocker*.

ARNOLD: Don't you meet any men your own age?

MA: In Miami Beach? If he's not your friend why's he cooking your breakfast?

ARNOLD: You never cook for your friends?

MA: Not breakfast. Didn't you used to have a friend named Ed who got married?

ARNOLD: You've got a great tan.

MA: He's a teacher?

ARNOLD: And a great memory.

MA: The girl was, too, right? They've got a house in the country.

ARNOLD: Incredible.

MA: I remember thinking, "Now there'a a man with his head on straight." What's he doing cooking your breakfast?

ARNOLD: He and his wife have separated. He's staying here till he can find a place of his own.

MA: Separated? How come?

ARNOLD: I don't know.

MA: Come on, the man's living with you. He must've said something.

ARNOLD: I didn't ask and he didn't volunteer.

MA: You're involved?

ARNOLD: No!

MA: Arnold?

ARNOLD: Ma?

MA: So why's he staying here?

ARNOLD: Because he asked if he could and I said yes.

MA: You must admit, it sounds a little queer: A man leaves his wife to move in with his old . . . friend.

ARNOLD: He's spending a few nights on my couch. What's the big deal?

MA: No big deal. But, you'd think he'd stay by friends that have more in common.

ARNOLD: What does that mean?

MA: You know; someone he met after the marriage.

ARNOLD: Maybe he needed to get away from all of that.

MA: You mean he's still? . . . (*Makes a motion with her hand*)

ARNOLD: Can we talk about the weather now?

MA: I'm glad you reminded me. (*Heads for her shopping bag*) Your mother! If I didn't have my head screwed on . . . I baked you some cookies. (*Produces a tin*) Fresh from the Sunshiney State. Take a whiff; you can smell Miami.

ARNOLD: David'll love these.

MA: I didn't know what to bring. I hadn't seen the place to know what you need.

ARNOLD (*Friendly and confident now*):   Oh, I didn't show you. . . . (*Takes out an afghan*) Look what I'm making. I took a class in weaving and crocheting at night school. Isn't it beautiful?

MA: I'm telling you! . . .

ARNOLD: I made it for out here. Y'know, for taking a nap on the couch. I wanna make one for my bedroom too. You like it?

MA (*Trying to look away*):   Nice.

ARNOLD: Pretty design, huh?

MA: It's fairy nice.

ARNOLD (*The wind knocked out of him*):   Well, maybe you should unpack. You can put your things in my room.

MA: How are we arranging all of this?

ARNOLD: You'll sleep in my room, David in his room, and Ed and I can share the couch.

MA: Wouldn't it be easier if I slept on the couch? That way you'll have your privacy.

ARNOLD: We don't need privacy.

MA: How about if you shared David's room?

ARNOLD: Did you see my cigarettes around?

MA: You still smoke? Shame on you. (*Arnold heaves a heavy sigh.*) What's the matter, *shayner boyalah*? You didn't sleep good?

ARNOLD: I'm fine. Just give me a minute to get myself together.

MA: Go on, get yourself together. I could use a get-together myself. (*Deep breath*) Arnold, where's the dog? He didn't come to say hello.

ARNOLD: I had to give him away. He used to sit by the door and whine all day and night, waiting for Alan to come home. I couldn't take it so I gave him to Murray. (*Referring to stack of papers she has unpacked*) What's all that?

MA: Don't ask me why, they forwarded some of your mail to me.

ARNOLD: Anything I should know about?

MA: Garbage. But there's a letter from Ernie the insurance man. You canceled your policy?

ARNOLD: One of them.

MA: You need money? You know I'm always good for a loan.

ARNOLD: Thanks but things are fine.

MA: Meanwhile you lost out on a very good deal. You wouldn't see a policy like that again.

ARNOLD: What do I need with a twenty-five-thousand-dollar life insurance policy?

MA: Now you don't need it, but someday? . . . You never know; you might meet a nice girl . . .

ARNOLD: Maaaa!

MA: You never know. Look at your friend Ed.

ARNOLD: I'm looking. He's separated.

MA: Separated, but not divorced. Believe me, you never know.

ARNOLD: Believe me. I know.

MA: What's the matter; you don't want children?

ARNOLD: Not the kind you mean.

MA: The kind I mean have two arms, two legs, a mother, father, and Chicken Pox. How many kinds are there?

ARNOLD: You'd be surprised.

MA: Arnold, you and your brother are the last of the Beckoffs.

ARNOLD: So?

MA: Don't you feel you have a duty to continue the family name?

ARNOLD: Not particularly. Anyway, there's always my brother. I'm sure there'll be lots of little Beckoffs running around.

MA: And what if he only has girls?

ARNOLD (*Thinks a moment*):   I know a good surgeon.

MA: I don't get you.

ARNOLD: Why don't you unpack while I take a shower and shave. And when I'm dressed we can sit and have a lonng talk.

MA: A "lonnng" talk? I feel a gray hair growing in.

ARNOLD: It's not that bad. Let me help with your bags.

MA: I can manage.

ARNOLD: It's the room on the right. Shit, I didn't have time to make the bed.

MA: Take your shower. I'll do it.

ARNOLD: There's fresh linen in the closet at the end of the hall.

MA (*Waving him on*):   Go. I'll get by.

ARNOLD: I won't be long. (*Exits*)

MA (*Gathering her things*):   You see, Jack? They still need the old mama. (*Exiting*) Just think, if I wasn't here . . . who would make the beds?
(*David enters through the front door, slowly, peeking in first. Seeing a deserted room, he enters fully and looks around. He spots the shopping bag.*)

DAVID: She has arrived. But where are she? (*Looks in kitchen, under table, goes to bathroom door, and listens*) We got us a live one. (*Arnold hums a bit of something.*) Wrong one. (*He is having fun. He tiptoes to the hall and exits. . . . A moment of silence, then a shriek. David runs out of the hall pursued by Ma, who is swinging at him with her purse.*) Mrs. Beckoff, please. I'm not a burglar!

MA: Then what are you; some kind of weirdo who gets a kick watching middle-aged women strip beds?

DAVID: I'm not a weirdo. Believe me.

MA: Then you're a rapist. (*She screams again.*)

DAVID: What would a rapist be doing in a three-piece suit?

MA: How should I know? Maybe you got a wedding after.

ARNOLD (*Entering, dripping in a robe*):   What the . . . David! What are you doing out of school?

MA: This is your roommate?

DAVID: Charmed, I'm sure.

MA: You know that "lonnng" talk we're gonna have? It just got lonnnnnnnger.

ARNOLD: What are you doing home?

DAVID: I forgot, I had a double period of gym and no uniform. So I tole Mr. Kelley about your mother comin' and he said I could come home till after lunch.

ARNOLD: Just like that?

DAVID: Well . . . you gotta call and say it's okay. Wasn't that nice of him?

ARNOLD (*Sees his mother's puzzled face*):   We'll discuss this later. (*Trying to smile*) Ma, this is David.

MA: So I gathered.

ARNOLD (*Long uncomfortable pause*):   Okay. So, now we all know each other.

MA: Arnold, you're dripping on my shoe.

ARNOLD: Oh. How about this: You go finish unpacking, I'll go finish my shower, and you go start lunch . . . ?

DAVID: It's only nine o'clock.

ARNOLD (*Parental order*):   When I tell you to do some-thing . . . (*Catches Ma staring*) Well, I'm going to dry off now.

MA: You do that.

ARNOLD (*Slowly backing out*):   So, you'll unpack, right? You'll make lunch, right? And I'll . . .

MA: Dry up.

ARNOLD: Right. (*Takes a last look, crosses himself, and exits*)

DAVID (*Pause*):   Would you like a drink?

MA: Maybe later. I'm sorry I hit you.

DAVID: No sweat. I usually charge, but seein' how you're family . . . (*He laughs.*)

MA: You have quite a little sense of humor. Shall we sit down?

DAVID: Sure. (*They do.*)

MA: Tell me, David, you go to school?

DAVID: Yeah. (*Sees cookies*) You make these?

MA: Help yourself. (*He does, by the handful.*) So, you go to college.

DAVID: High school.

MA (*Her heart!*):   High school. How nice. (*Hopeful*) Senior year?

DAVID: Freshman.

MA: That's very sweet. Tell me, David, just how old are you?

DAVID: Sixteen . . . in two months. (*Sees her dying*) Something wrong?

MA: Not at all. Sixteen . . . in two months . . . that's wonderful. You have your whole life ahead of you . . . while mine's flashing before my eyes.

DAVID (*Chomping away*):   Good stuff.

MA (*At first she thinks he referred to her life, then . . .*):   Thank you. David, it's none of my business, of course, but don't you think you're a little young to be out in the world all alone?

DAVID: No. But, the judge did, so here I am.

ARNOLD (*Sticking his head out*):   Everything all right out here?

MA (*Choking*):   Fine, dear. Keep drying. (*Arnold withdraws.*)

DAVID: You like the place? We cleaned all week for you. Sorry I didn't get back to see your face when you got here.

MA: That face couldn't compare to this one.

DAVID: I woulda taken the whole morning off, but you know Arnold. . . . Hey, he better hurry up and call the school. Mr. Kelley'll think I was jivin' him.

MA: Does Arnold make all your excuses at school?

DAVID (*Enjoying the game*):   Sure. Who else?

MA: Who else, indeed. I've got an idea: Why don't I call the school while you change your clothes?

DAVID: Hey, I wore this special for you.

MA: I've seen it, it's cute, now put it away.

DAVID: Yeah, but . . .

MA (*Pointing*):   March.

DAVID (*Exiting*):   Now I know where Arnold got his technique.

MA: Cute kid. (*Calling out*) David? Where do you keep the phone numbers?

DAVID (*Off*):   In the phone book.

MA: A little too cute. *Oy,* Arnold, what have you got yourself into now? (*Finds book*) Here it is. Right on top. Must get used a lot. (*Starts to dial . . .*) David? What name shall I give them?

DAVID: What?

MA: Who shall I say is being excused? (*No response*) Your last name!

DAVID (*Sticking his head in*):   Beckoff, of course.

MA: Really? That's quite a coincidence. Have you and Arnold ever compared notes to see if there's any family relation?

DAVID: I'm his son. What more relation could there be? (*Arnold steps out of the bathroom.*)

MA: You're his what?

DAVID: His son. (*Arnold goes right back into the bathroom.*) Would you like that drink now?

The lights black out; music plays in the dark for a moment. It should be the Hartz Mountain Canaries singing "The Blue Danube Waltz."

SCENE TWO

Later that afternoon. The stage is exactly as it was before (except deserted). Ed lets himself in with his key. He enters carrying a small paper bag and newspaper.

ED: Hello? Anybody home?
A platter flies across the room from the hallway and just misses his head, smashing on the wall. It is followed by Arnold.

ARNOLD: Deserter! Defector! Duty-dodger! Ditching your post at the first sign of battle, you backstabbing, betraying, ball-breaking Buttercup! How could you leave me unprotected? You Avoider! Abstainer! Abandoner! Absconderer!

ED: Absconderer?

ARNOLD: If the shoe fits . . . Where have you been?

ED: Buying milk.

ARNOLD: For nine hours?

ED: I was on the express line. What happened?

ARNOLD: Happened? What could possibly have happened? My mother walked through that door and within three minutes managed to insult the plane ride, the bus ride, Women's Lib, the apartment, Manhattan, my personal hygiene, sense of humor, afghan, smoking, stenciling, and cockroaches. And, oh, you'll love this: She accused me of breaking up your marriage.

ED: You're kidding.

ARNOLD: She practically called me a homewrecker. Okay, so far so good. We finally sat down to chat when who should walk through the door, but the Patron Saint of Truants himself: Champ David. My mother gets a gander at him and goes,

"What a sweet child. And whose little boy are you?" Giving
the long-awaited cue to my sweet little angel lamb to turncoat
'round and point his every available finger at me.

ED: Oops.

ARNOLD: Did you say "Oops"? No, Ed. "Oops" is when you fall
down an elevator shaft. "Oops" is when you skinny-dip in a
school of piranha. "Oops" is for accidentally douching with
Drāno. No, Ed, this was not an "Oops." This was a (*Strangled
Scream*)!

ED: Cut the dramatics and tell me what happened.

ARNOLD: I'm telling you, nothing happened.

ED: Nothing?

ARNOLD: As in "Not a thing." Dear David went atwitter to his
room, mother went to my room, and I sat in the bathroom
making toilet-paper flowers and flushing them down the drain.
Three hours I flowered and flushed, flowered and flushed,
till, Thank God, I ran out of paper. Forced from my Autumn
Beige Tiled retreat, I called a truce for lunch. It was eaten in
silence. No one even chewed. (You ever gum down a ham-
burger?) After lunch David announced he was going back to
school and my mother volunteered to walk him.

ED: Where are they now?

ARNOLD: I haven't the smoggiest. Knowing David, he's probably
fuming over some pinball machine. I was gonna look for him
but it's better if he makes it home on his own.

ED: That's very sensible.

ARNOLD: Not at all. But what would I say if I did find him. And
the mother . . . I don't know where she could be.

ED: "Leave them alone and they'll come home . . ."

ARNOLD: ". . . dragging a noose behind them." Help me with
dinner.

ED: A quick trip to the men's room and I'll set the table.

ARNOLD: You'll have to borrow a plunger from next door, first. A thousand sheets really do last longer. (*Picking up the broken china*) Look at this, you broke my favorite platter.

ED: I broke?

ARNOLD: Come on, get going. And don't go disappearing on me again.

ED: I'll be right back. (*Exits*)
(*The phone rings. Arnold rushes to it.*)

ARNOLD: Hello? . . . Oh, hi, Murray. . . . No, I've been home all day. . . . Because I was in the bathroom. . . . Yes, all day. You wanna sue me? . . . Look, Murr, I ain't got time to tear a herring with you now. You got somethin' to say? Say it. . . . Rocco who? Rocco DiGemma? The one with the Leatherette T-shirts? . . . Yeah, I know him. What about him? . . . You told him I'd do what?!!!? . . . Uh-huh. . . . Uh-huh. . . . Uh-huh. . . . Uh-huh . . . and then? . . . Uh-huh. . . . Uh-huh. . . . Uh-huh. . . . Uh-huh. . . . Uh-huh. . . . Listen, Marie, (*At this point Ma and David enter happily*) you can call that poor excuse for a rubber creep back and tell him . . . (*He sees them*) . . . tell him I've got a previous engagement. Thanks for calling. Bye-bye. (*Hangs up*)

MA (*Removing her jacket*):   Who was that, dear?

ARNOLD (*Puzzled*):   It was Murray. He wanted me to do a favor for a friend.

MA: What did he want you to do?

ARNOLD: . . . Baby-sit. You were together?

DAVID: I took your mother to school with me.

MA: They were very nice. They let me sit in the back. He does very well; when he stays awake.

DAVID: Then I took her to play pinball.

MA: You weren't worried, were you?

ARNOLD: What, me worry?

DAVID: Hey, Alfred E., what's for dinner? (*Heads to kitchen*)

MA: Would you like to go out? My treat.

ARNOLD: I've started dinner here. But if you'd rather . . .

MA: No, we'll go out tomorrow. Besides, my feet are screaming for my slippers.

ED (*Enters with plunger*):   Well, look who's here.

MA: Hello, Ed. How was your day?

ED: Fine . . . thank you, Mrs. Beckoff. And yours?

MA: Surprisingly pleasant, once it was settled into. (*Exiting. To David*) After you do your homework I'll teach you how to play chess.

DAVID (*With a can of soda*):   Homework? Is she kidding? Hey, Arnold, we got a chess set?

ARNOLD: Top shelf of your closet.

DAVID: Thanks. Hi, Ed. (*Exits*)

ED: And you were worried. (*Goes toward bathroom*)

ARNOLD: I wasn't worried. I was concerned. (*Ed exits.*)

MA (*Enters in bunny slippers like Arnold's*):   Give me an apron and put me to work.

ARNOLD: That's all right, Ma. Ed's gonna help.

MA: Oh, I wondered what the plunger was for. Listen, if I'm gonna die of ptomaine, it'll be from something I made myself. (*Holding up a potato*) What do you want done with these?

ARNOLD: I was going to bake them, but if I could twist your arm? . . .

MA: You want my *Latkes*?

ARNOLD: I'd love your *Latkes*.

MA: Then you'll get my *Latkes*.

ED (*Entering*):   All fixed.

ARNOLD: Thanks, Ed.

DAVID (*Off*):   Hey, Arnold? I can't find the chessboard.

ARNOLD: Coming. (*Exits*) Be back.

MA (*Trying to draw Ed in*):   You like *Latkes*, Ed?

ED: I don't know. I never had it.

MA: Them. You're in for a treat.

ED: I couldn't help noticing, you've got slippers like Arnold's.
Mind if I ask who gave them to whom?

MA (*Modeling them*):   You like my slippers? Aren't they Chick?
Arnold gave them to me. You know what they say; in matters
of taste, there is none.

ED: I see where Arnold gets his wit.

MA: That and his appetite are from me. But the face? He's his
father's son. He's got his heart too. Always a soft touch. Tell
me, Ed, what do you think of Arnold taking in this boy?

ED: I think it's wonderful.

MA: You do? Frankly, I'm not wild for it. But look, it's only for
a few more weeks, so what harm could it do?

ED: Oops.

MA (*Calling to Arnold*):   Arnold? You have Matzo Meal?

ARNOLD (*Enters*):   Yeah, I'll get it for you.

MA (*Proud*):   He has Matzo Meal. Did I bring him up right?
(*David enters with a book, sits down on the couch, and begins
to read.*)

ARNOLD: Here you go, Ma. You need eggs?

MA: Two, please. And an onion?

ED (*Looking agog at David*): Are you doing homework?

DAVID: Nah. I'm just readin' somethin' from school.

MA: Arnold's father used to love my *Latkes*. But his favorite was my Potato Soup. You remember how he liked it, Arnold?

ARNOLD: I remember.

MA: It wasn't potato soup like you think; made with vegetables and cream. What he liked was: You took a potato, boiled it in water, threw in a *bissel* salt and pepper and that was Potato Soup. Arnold used to call it "Daddy's Potato Water." You remember?

ARNOLD: Yes, Ma.

MA: We were Depression babies. You understand? Whether you have to or not, you carry that through your life. The tastes, the smells . . . they bring back a cozy feeling of a time you don't quite remember. You know what I'm talking?

ED: I think so.

MA: Good. 'Cause I don't. (*Arnold hugs her.*) What's that for?

ARNOLD: I'm glad you're here.

MA: Me too, *Tatalah*.

ED (*To David*): I didn't know you could read.

DAVID: I just look at the pictures.

ED: What is it?

DAVID: Some garbage for English.

ED: What?

DAVID: A poem. I don't know. (*Reading and mispronouncing the word "Gaol"*) "The Ballad of Reading Gaol" by Oscar Wilde.

ED (*Correcting*): That's gaol, like in j-a-i-l.

DAVID: That ain't what it says.

ED: That's the British spelling.

ARNOLD: (*From memory*)
"Yet each man kills the thing he loves,
By each let this be heard,
Some do it with a bitter look, Some with a flattering word.
The coward does it with a kiss,
The brave man with a sword!"

ED: Very good.

MA: What? You think I raised a dope?

ARNOLD: We had to learn it in high school. Y'know, I still get shivers when I think of that poor man going through all that pain and torment just to write a cliché.

DAVID: What's a cliché?

ARNOLD: The sincerest form of flattery.

DAVID (*To Ed*): Was that a joke?

ARNOLD (*Coming out of kitchen*): Did your teacher happen to mention how Oscar Wilde came to be imprisoned?

DAVID: Maybe. Who listens?

ARNOLD: He was in jail for being gay.

DAVID: No, I think I woulda remembered that.

MA (*Embarrassed*): Arnold, I can't find the oil.

ARNOLD: In a minute, Ma. See, ten years earlier, the Parliament passed a law against homosexuality. And Oscar Wilde had this young lover named . . .

MA: Arnold, could you please give me a hand?

ARNOLD: Just a second. His name was Lord Alfred.

DAVID: Royalty, huh?

ED (*To Ma*): Anything I can help you with?

MA: No, thank you, Ed.

ARNOLD: Now, Lord Alfred's father found out about them and started causing scenes in public; chasin' 'em outta hotels and stuff. But the straw that broke the dam was a note sent to Wilde's hotel. It said, "To Oscar Wilde, who poses as a Sodomite."

MA: For God's sake, Arnold. Could you change the subject?

ARNOLD (*Annoyed*): I'll finish later. (*Goes back to kitchen*)

ED: Here, we'll read the poem together and I'll explain anything you don't understand.

DAVID: I want the rest of the dish. (*Ed kicks him.*) Ouch, that hurt.
(David and Ed read quietly and we hear the conversation from the kitchen.)

ARNOLD: I wish you wouldn't interfere like that; it's very embarrassing.

MA: Excuse me, but listening to that is very embarrassing.

ARNOLD: I'm sorry you feel that way, but I have a responsibility to his education.

MA: I am sure that the people who put him here did not have that kind of education in mind.

ARNOLD: The people who put him here had exactly that kind of education in mind. And I'll thank you not to interfere.

MA: I am only suggesting that you should consider the huge responsibility you've taken on here.

ARNOLD: You think I'm unaware of it?

MA: Then act like it. You should be setting an example for the boy.

ARNOLD: And I'm not?

MA: Not when you talk like that, you're not. You've got to

consider what you say to him for the remaining time. He's at an impressionable age. After all, it's only for a few more months.

ARNOLD (*Ed and David stop.*):   What's for a few more months?

MA: He's here on a nine-month program, right? And he's already been here six months, so . . .

ARNOLD: And what do you think happens then?

MA: He leaves.

DAVID: No, you misunderstoo— (*Ed kicks him again.*) Ow! This is getting serious.

ARNOLD: There seems to be a misinterpretation afoot. Yes, David is here on a nine-month program, but after that, if we agree and the Bureau of Child Welfare allows, I will legally adopt David. And believe me, Ma, if I have anything to say about it, he's not leaving.
(*Ma tries to say something, she is angry, confused, frustrated. She throws down whatever is in her hands and storms out. We hear the door slam.*)

ARNOLD: That was an "Oops."

ED: I thought so.

ARNOLD (*To David*):   What'd you tell her?

DAVID: I didn't say nothin'.

ARNOLD: You certainly got a way without words. Well, kids, wish me luck.

DAVID: You goin' in there?

ARNOLD: Anybody got any suggestions?

DAVID: Don't look at me.

ED: Sorry, I'm just the baby-sitter.

ARNOLD: Somber times inspire your whimsicality. I'll remember that.

ED: And don't forget to write.

DAVID: We'll be in the next room; so talk loud.

ARNOLD: Thanks. (*Deep breath*) Well, here goes everything.
(*He exits, we hear a knock on the door, then the door opens
and closes. Ed and David jump up and rush to hallway.*)

DAVID: You hear anything?

ED: Shhhhhhh.

DAVID (*Going to kitchen*): Ah, he stalled too long. They're gonna
need time to warm up again. Let's eat.

ED: I can't hear a thing. This is ridiculous; a grown man listening at a hallway. I should go right up to the door. (*He exits.*)

DAVID (*Shouting*): You want a sandwich?

ED (*Runs back in*): Could you not yell like that?

DAVID (*Whispers*): Hear anything?

ED: No.

DAVID: Told ya. Have a sandwich. We'll know when they get
goin'.

ED: You're taking this very calmly. I'm more curious than you,
it seems.

DAVID: Looks that way, don't it.

ED: What'd you tell her, anyway?

DAVID: A little of this, a little of that. What's the difference?
You know how it is with grown-ups: They only hear what they
wanna. (*He listens.*) Hang on, we're about to get a bulletin.
(*Ma enters as if she rushed away. She sits on couch. Arnold
follows and stands staring at her.*)

DAVID: Care to repose and repast?

ED (*Grabs David*): Come on, Kissinger. I'll teach you how to play
chess.

DAVID: Wait, my sandwich.

ED (*Pulling him off*): You'll concentrate better on an empty stomach.

ARNOLD (*Sits next to her. Pause.*): Is this it? We gonna sit and stare into space?

MA: You want I should do a Bubble Dance?

ARNOLD: I need a cigarette. (*He gets one.*)

MA: Frankly, Arnold, you've done a lot of crazy things, but this? . . .

ARNOLD: Adopting David is not a crazy thing. It's a wonderful thing that I'm very proud of.

MA: If you're so proud how come you were too ashamed to tell your mother? Everything else you tell me. You shove your sex life down my throat like aspirin, every hour on the hour. But six months he's been here and not a word. Why?

ARNOLD: I don't know.

MA: So what's new?

ARNOLD: Ma . . . y'know, you're not the easiest person in the world to talk to.

MA: What did I say? Do I tell you how to run your life? Let me tell you something, my son: I learned long ago that no matter what I said or how I felt, you and your brother were going to do just as you pleased anyway. So, I wouldn't say a word. On purpose! You want to know why you didn't tell me about this? I'll tell you why: Because you knew it was wrong.

ARNOLD: That's not true.

MA: No?

ARNOLD: No!

MA: Why then?

ARNOLD: . . . I don't know.

MA: You would if you'd listened.

ARNOLD: This isn't something I decided to do overnight. We put in our application more than two years ago.

MA: Who "we"?

ARNOLD: Alan and I.

MA: The two of you were going to do this together?

ARNOLD: That was the idea.

MA: Now I've heard everything.

ARNOLD: That's what I love about you; you're so open-minded.

MA: All right. So, Alan's not here. Why's the kid?

ARNOLD: Because with everything else I forgot about the application. Then, one day, the phone rang. It was the foster parent program and they had David for us. I told them what happened to Alan and they said I could probably take David anyway.

MA: And you said, "Send him on over."

ARNOLD: Not at first. But then I thought it all through, called them back, and said yes . . . on a trial basis.

MA: I'm glad you got a money-back guarantee, but you still haven't told me why you wanted him.

ARNOLD: Because I was tired of widowing.

MA: Wida-whating?

ARNOLD: Widowing. Widow-ing. It's a word of Murray's.

MA: And a nice one at that. What does it mean?

ARNOLD: You know.

MA: No, I don't know.

ARNOLD: Widowing . . . feeling sorry for myself, cursing every time I passed a couple walking hand in hand, watching Tear-

jerkers on TV, knowing they could only cheer me up. Christ, of all the things going down here, I was sure that was the one thing I wouldn't have to explain.

MA: How should I know about Whatchamacallit? Did you ever say a word to me?

ARNOLD: I didn't think I had to. Christ, it's only been three years since Daddy died.

MA: Wait, wait, wait, wait, wait. Are you trying to compare my marriage with you and Alan? (*Haughty and incensed*) Your father and I were married for thirty-five years, had two children and a wonderful life together. You have the nerve to compare yourself to that?

ARNOLD (*Scared*): That's not what I mean, I'm talking about the loss.

MA: What loss did you have? You fooled around with some boy . . . ? Where do you come to compare that to a marriage of thirty-five years?

ARNOLD: You think it doesn't?

MA: Come on, Arnold. You think you're talking to one of your pals?

ARNOLD: Ma, I lost someone that I loved very much . . .

MA: So you felt bad. Maybe you cried a little. But what would you know about what I went through? Thirty-five years I lived with that man. He got sick, I brought him to the hospital, and you know what they gave me back? I gave them a man . . . they gave me a paper bag with his watch, wallet, and wedding ring. How could you possibly know what that felt like. It took me two months until I could sleep in our bed alone, a year to learn to say "I" instead of "we." And you're going to tell me you were "widowing." How dare you!

ARNOLD: You're right, Ma. How dare I. I couldn't possibly know how it feels to pack someone's clothes in plastic bags and watch the garbage-pickers carry them away. Or what it feels like to

forget and set his place at the table. How about the food that rots in the refrigerator because you forgot how to shop for one? How dare I? Right, Ma? How dare I?

MA (*Starting over his speech and continuing until her exit*):   May God strike me dead! Whatever I did to my mother to deserve a child speaking to me this way. The disrespect! I only pray that one day you have a son and that he'll talk to you like this. The way you talk to me.

ARNOLD (*Over her speech*):   Listen, Ma, you had it easy. You have thirty-five years to remember, I have five. You had your children and friends to comfort you, I had me! My friends didn't want to hear about it. They said, "What're you gripin' about? At least you had a lover." 'Cause everybody knows that queers don't feel nothin'. How dare I say I loved him? You had it easy, Ma. You lost your husband in a nice clean hospital, I lost mine out there. They killed him there on the street. Twenty-three years old, laying dead on the street. Killed by a bunch of kids with baseball bats. (*Ma has fled the room. Arnold continues to rant.*) Children. Children taught by people like you. 'Cause everybody knows that queers don't matter! Queers don't love! And those that do deserve what they get! (*He stops, catches his breath, sits down.*) Whatever happened to good ole American Momism and apple pie?

DAVID (*Sticking his head out from the hall*):   Could you keep it down? There's people tryin' to concentrate.

ARNOLD (*Laughing*):   Sorry.

DAVID: Round one over?

ARNOLD: I really lost control. I didn't mean to say any of that. But it came pouring out; I felt like I was fighting for my life.

DAVID (*Coming close*):   This is highly flattering: A duel to the death over li'l ole me.

ARNOLD: Don't overdramatize. I do enough of that for both of us.

DAVID (*Hug*):   I think you're wonderful.

ARNOLD: Where's Uncle Ed?

ED (*Sticking his head out*):   Present. Is round one over?

ARNOLD: We've called a cease-fire to regroup.

DAVID: Can we eat now?

ARNOLD: Why don't you two go out for something?

ED: How about you?

ARNOLD: Don't know why, but I ain't hungry. Go on.

ED: You're not going back in there, are you?

ARNOLD: I can't leave things like this.

ED: You're very brave.

ARNOLD: I'm very stupid. None of this would've happened if I'd been honest all along.

ED: Or dishonest all along.

ARNOLD: That's not for me. Get going.

ED (*Intimate*):   Let me stay. We can all talk together.

DAVID: You want us to bring something back for you?

ARNOLD (*To David*):   No, thanks. (*To Ed*) No, thanks.

DAVID (*His jacket on*):   Put a candle in the window when it's clear to come home. We'll wait on the bench.

ARNOLD (*Hugging him*):   I'll do that.

ED (*At the door*):   What'll it be; pizza?

DAVID: You paying?

ED: Sure.

DAVID: Then I know this intimate little French restaurant . . . (*Exit*)

ARNOLD (*Takes a deep breath*):   Round two. (*Sits on couch, feet up*) Yoo-hoo, Mrs. Bloom! It's safe to come out. David and Ed went for a walk and we've got the whole place to fight in.

MA (*Off*):   Enjoy yourself. I'm going to bed.

ARNOLD: Ma, I'm sorry I lost my temper.

MA: Ha! I'm glad you're sorry.

ARNOLD: Please come out here. We can't talk like this.

MA (*In doorway*):   You don't want to talk, you want to fight. But I don't fight with my children. In your life did you ever hear your father and I fight? No. And do you know why? I'll tell you why: Because all my childhood I listened to fights. My father fought with my mother, my mother fought with my brother, my mother fought with me. . . . When I married your father I told him, "Jack, I'll talk, but I won't fight." And did you ever hear us fight? No. And now you know why.

ARNOLD: You wanna sit down?

MA (*Wandering over to the couch*):   I'm sitting.

ARNOLD: All right. . . .

MA (*Warning*):   And don't holler at me. People say things they don't mean when they holler and you've already said quite enough.

ARNOLD: I won't holler. You just hit a raw nerve. We won't discuss Alan. Only David.

MA: So discuss.

ARNOLD: Why don't you tell me what you already know, and we'll go on from there.

MA (*Trying*):   I don't know anything.

ARNOLD: You spent the day with him. He must've said something.

MA: Let me think. He's an orphan . . .

ARNOLD: He's not an orphan.

MA: He said he was an orphan.

ARNOLD: Well, he's not. He was a battered child. They took him away from his parents. This is his third foster home. The first brought him back. The second he ran away from. So . . .

MA: So, he's a liar.

ARNOLD: He's not a liar . . .

MA: This isn't going to work.

ARNOLD: Come on, we're finally getting somewhere. . . .

MA: How do you expect me to sit here and discuss this insanity?

ARNOLD: You're right, this isn't going to work.

MA: Arnold, Arnold, what do you know from raising a child?

ARNOLD: What's to know? Whenever I have a problem I simply imagine how you would solve it, and do the opposite.

MA (*Standing*):   Is this what you invited me up here for? To insult me and spit on your father's grave?

ARNOLD: For cryin' out . . . will you please sit down?

MA (*Sitting*):   Don't holler. I'm sitting. I don't know why, but I'm sitting.

ARNOLD: All right. Now we're going to talk about David. Not Alan, not Daddy, just David. And we're going to stay calm.

MA: Ha!

ARNOLD: I give up.

MA: Arnold, darling, open your eyes. Don't you see how ridiculous this is? I've been here less than a day, already I've seen you let him miss school, hang out on the street, go out without dinner . . .

ARNOLD: This is hardly a typical day.

MA: You wanna talk or make excuses?

ARNOLD: This isn't Little Lord Fauntleroy we're talking about here. If this kid decided I was coming down too hard on him, he'd pack and take off and I'd never get him back again. That sweet-looking little boy knows how to make more money in a night than you and I could make in a week.

MA: So you let him run wild?

ARNOLD: No. But I don't beat him up either. I teach him. I advise him, I try to set an example for him . . .

MA: Some example. Arnold, look, you live the life you want. I put my fist in my mouth, I don't say a word. This is what you want. But think about the boy. He likes you. He told me he loves you. He sees you living like this . . . don't you think it's going to affect him?

ARNOLD: Ma, David is gay.

MA: But he's only been here six months!

ARNOLD: He came that way.

MA: No one comes that way.

ARNOLD: What an opening.

MA: By you everything is a joke.

ARNOLD: Don't you understand: The whole purpose of placing him here was for him to grow up with a positive attitude about his homosexuality.

MA: That's it. (*Stands*) I'm finished. The world has gone completely mad and I'm heading South for the summer.

ARNOLD: You make it very difficult to have an intelligent conversation.

MA: You want an intelligent conversation? Do what I do: Talk to yourself. It's the only way.

ARNOLD: You think this is easy for me? Look; my hands are

shaking. I've been like this for days, knowing you'd be coming and we'd have to talk about this.

MA: Because you knew I'd show you how wrong you are.

ARNOLD: I'm not wrong.

MA: No? Tell me something: How old was your friend Alan when you met him?

ARNOLD: Seventeen.

MA: Seventeen. Seventeen and you were doing God knows what together. Now, tell me; how old is this "son" of yours?

ARNOLD: I have no intention of sleeping with him if that's what you're driving at.

MA: I had no intention of having a homosexual for a son. So, look where intentions get you. Arnold, do what you want. You want to live like this? *Gay gezzintah hait.* I don't care anymore. You're not going to make me sick like you did your father.

ARNOLD: I made my father sick?

MA: No; he was thrilled to have a fairy for a son! You took a lifetime of dreams and threw them back in his face.

ARNOLD: What lifetime of dreams? He knew I was gay for four-teen years.

MA: What? You think you walk into a room, say, "Hi, Dad, I'm queer," and that's that? You think that's what we brought you into the world for? Believe me, if I'd known I wouldn't have bothered. God should tear out my tongue, I should talk to my child this way. Arnold, you're my son, you're a good person, a sensitive person with a heart, *kennohorrah*, like your father and I try to love you for that and forget this. But you won't let me. You've got to throw me on the ground and rub my face in it. You haven't spoken a sentence since I got here without the word "Gay" in it.

ARNOLD: Because that's what I am.

MA: If that were all you could leave it in there (*Points to bedroom*) where it belongs; in private. No, you're obsessed by it. You're not happy unless everyone is talking about it. I don't know why you don't just wear a big sign and get it over with.

ARNOLD (*Bordering on hysteria*):   I don't know what to say to you. I really don't. I'm not trying to throw it in your face but it is what I am and it's not just a matter of who I sleep with. (*Crosses to her*) Ma, try to imagine the world the other way around. Imagine that every movie, book, magazine, TV show, newspaper, commercial, billboard, told you that you should be homosexual. But you know you're not and you know that for you this is right . . .

MA: Arnold, stop already. You're talking crazy.

ARNOLD: You want to know what's crazy? That after all these years I'm still here justifying my life. That's what's crazy.

MA: You call this a life? This is a sickness! But this is what you've chosen for yourself.

ARNOLD (*Deep breath, one last try*):   Ma, look: I'm gay. I don't know why. I don't think anyone does. But that's what I am. For as far back as I can remember. Back before I knew it was different or wrong . . .

MA: You have not heard a word I've said.

ARNOLD (*Losing control*):   I know you'd rather I was straight but I am not! Would you also rather I had lied to you? My friends all think I'm crazy for telling you. They'd never dream of telling their parents. Instead they cut their parents out of their lives. And the parents wonder, "Why are my children so distant?" Is this what you'd rather?

MA: But it doesn't have to be our every conversation either.

ARNOLD: You want a part in my life? I am not going to edit out the things you don't like!

MA (*Scared*):   Can we end this conversation?

ARNOLD: No. There's one more thing you've got to understand. You made fun of my crocheting before. You think it's a cute little effeminate thing I do. Let me tell you something; I have taught myself to sew, cook, fix plumbing, do taxes, build furniture. . . . I can even pat myself on the back when necessary. All so I don't have to ask anyone for anything. There is nothing I need from anyone except love and respect. And anyone who can't give me those two things has no place in my life. (*Breath*) You are my mother, and I love you. I do. But if you can't respect me . . . then you've got no business being here.

MA: You're throwing me out?

ARNOLD: What I'm trying to . . .

MA: You're throwing me out! Isn't that nice? Listen, Mister, you get one mother in this world. Only one. Wait. Just you wait.

(*Ma exits to bedroom. Arnold is still as the next scene begins. The lights slowly crossfade.*)

SCENE THREE

A bench in the park below. Immediately following. If possible the bench should be played on the couch. Through the use of gobos and projections it is conceivable to create the nighttime park atmosphere on the apartment set. David and Ed enter talking, eating hot dogs.

DAVID: How's your hot dog, Big Spender?

ED: Been years since I bought one of these off the street. I just remembered why.

DAVID: Teach you to forget your wallet. (*David sits on bench.*)

ED: C'mon, lazy. I gotta walk this thing off.

DAVID: We're supposed to wait here. (*Pointing up*) Look. You can see our windows from here. Almost didn't take the apartment because of it.

ED: You lost me.

DAVID: Arnold never brung you here? This is where it happened.

ED: I didn't know.

DAVID: Yeah, here. They were walking back toward the street, Alan and the other guy, when the kids jumped out from behind these bushes. You can see; no way to run. Must've happened too quick anyway. Alan died right off, but the other guy crawled out to the street.

ED: I know.

DAVID: You can see a stain on the sidewalk in the daytime.

ED: Arnold showed you this?

DAVID: The day I moved in. At first I figured he was tryin' to scare me outta goin' into the park at night. I mean, I didn't

know him from shit and here he takes me out, first day, and shows me some dried-up blood on the sidewalk. I figured him for a nut-case. Like maybe he had a case against the world or somethin'. I mean, havin' a bunch of piss-offs take out your lover for kicks. . . . I could understand him bein' crazy. So, I felt sorry for him, but just passed it off. Then about a week later we were watchin' the news on TV and there was this protest march; a bunch of Jews marchin' against Nazis. They had these signs that said "Never Again" and "We Remember." And I looked over at Arnold and he was like cryin' real soft, and just like that I connected. I knew why he showed me this.

ED: No candle in the window yet.

DAVID: Give 'em time, they got a lotta yellin' to catch up on.

ED: That's one thing I can do without hearing any more of today. I saw Laurel this afternoon.

DAVID: Oh, yeah? What'd she want?

ED (*Realizing to whom he's talking*): Oh, nothing.

DAVID: Sure.

ED: Really.

DAVID: You don't have to tell me.

ED: It was nothing. Really.

DAVID: Hey, it's cool. You don't have to tell me. It ain't like we're old friends or nothing. After all, what am I to you?

ED: It was nothing. She just wanted to know if I was thinking of coming back.

DAVID: And you told her no.

ED: How do you know?

DAVID: I know.

ED: Frankly, I haven't made up my mind yet.

DAVID: You won't go back.

ED: Can we change the subject?

DAVID: Sure. So, now that you and Laurel are washed up, you gonna start shoppin' around?

ED: Well, since I haven't yet decided, then I haven't yet decided.

DAVID: Don't think about it too long or you'll wind up like Arnold.

ED: And that's bad?

DAVID: Arnold goes out to work and shop. That's all and that ain't healthy.

ED: You say that like you mean it.

DAVID: Who knows more about sex and its effect on mental health than me? Got any idea how many couches I've been laid out on? (*Ed smirks.*) Psychiatrically speaking. Starting when they turned my folks in I've had Freudian Analysis, Primal Analysis, Gestalt Analysis, Handwriting Analysis, Scream Therapy, Dream Therapy, Aversion Therapy and est. When they finally ran outta cures to put me through, they stamped my file "Hopelessly Homo," shook my hand, wished me luck, and shipped me off to Arnold. So I picked up plenty of know-how on my journey down the "Leatherette Road."

ED: Knowing and doing are two different things. You're only fifteen.

DAVID: Guess you don't read *The New York Times*. Seems no matter how many petitions they sign, they just can't get God to raise the age of puberty to eighteen. Kids have sex. But that's another subject.

ED: It certainly is.

DAVID: Bottom line is, here's Arnold: Attractive, sensitive, intelligent, a great conversationalist, pretty good cook, and he's living like an old Italian widow.

ED: So?

DAVID: So it's time for a change. Don't you think?

ED: Maybe.

DAVID: Got any suggestions?

ED: None I'd care to discuss with a fifteen-year-old.

DAVID: And you called him a bigot? Look, I ain't askin' for no miracles. (*Though I must say I'd be proud to call you Daddy.*) I'm simply suggestin' you could both use a little T.E.N.

ED: T.E.N.?

DAVID: Tension-Easing Nookie. Sex is very therapeutic.

ED: So you've said.

DAVID: What do you say?
(*Arnold enters carrying two hot dogs like a wedding bouquet.*)

ARNOLD (*à la Kate Hepburn*): Hello, Mother. Hello, Father. The frankfurters are in bloom again. (*Examines them*) Such a strange flower. Suitable for any occasion. I wore one on my wedding day, and now I place them here in memory of something that has . . . I don't know when to stop, do I? I brought supplies.

ED (*Holding his stomach*): We had the same idea. They're poison.

DAVID (*Grabbing two*): And so unfilling.

ARNOLD: Found your wallet on the table. Thought you might be hungry.

DAVID: Round two over?

ARNOLD: Two, three, four, five . . .

DAVID: Who won?

ARNOLD: When I left we both knew who won. Now only Robert Browning does. Ed, would you mind if I spoke to Champ alone?

ED (*Embarrassed*): Oh, sure.

DAVID: No, stay. I want witnesses.

ED: It's okay. Is it clear on the front?

ARNOLD: Should be. Got your key?

ED (*Checks*):   Yeah. I'll see you both later, then.

ARNOLD: Thanks, Ed. (*He exits.*)

DAVID: That was lousy. He wanted to help.

ARNOLD: I don't need his help, thank you. (*Pause*) Things got pretty "padded cell" up there.

DAVID: Yeah? (*Aloof*)

ARNOLD: You had to sit here, didn't you? I'm sorry I didn't tell her about you before. But believe me, it's not 'cause I was ashamed.

DAVID: Glad to hear it.

ARNOLD: My mother has a certain picture of what I should be doing with my life, and it's very hard for her to adjust to all the curves I throw in.

DAVID: Forge on.

ARNOLD: All right. I knew that even if I told her about you, even before you came to live with me, that sooner or later we'd have this showdown. It has nothing to do with you. It's just her last go-for-broke campaign to straighten out my life.

DAVID: And?

ARNOLD: I asked her to leave.

DAVID: You're good at that.

ARNOLD: But you've got to understand that whatever happens between my mother and me has nothing to do with us.

DAVID: Come on, Arnold. This ain't Ed you're talking to. Whatever goes down with you two is exactly what will happen with us.

ARNOLD: How do you figure that?

DAVID: 'Cause you're just like her.

ARNOLD: You wouldn't say that if you'd heard what went on up there.

DAVID: I know what goes on with mothers. Remember, you're my fourth. You think it's different 'cause we're both gay. But it's the same trip.

ARNOLD: No offense, Angel-Puss, but you're mistaken.

DAVID: Think so? What would you do if I met a girl, came home, and told you I was straight?

ARNOLD: If you were happy, I'd be happy.

DAVID: Bull-China! Here you are, workin' your butt off showin' me all the joys of gay life, givin' me the line of dignity and self-respect. . . . You tellin' me you wouldn't wonder where you went wrong?

ARNOLD: Not if you were sure that that's what you wanted.

DAVID: Yeah, I see the way you treat Ed. The guy keeps tellin' you he's Bi and all you keep doin' is callin' him a Closet Case.

ARNOLD: See, you don't know what you're talking about. I'd be perfectly willing to believe he's bi if just once he thought about the person he was with before he considered what sex that person was.

DAVID: How could anybody do that? You ever meet someone and not know what sex they were?

ARNOLD: That's not what I mean . . .

DAVID: I know what you mean and it's just as dumb. (*Arnold tries to speak.*) Shut up and let me finish. I stay with you because I want to. Dig? I really like living with you. I even like the way you try to mother me. But you can really be a shithead about things. But, you make me feel like I got a home. And a bunch of other assorted mushy stuff I don't want to get into here.

But, Arnold, I'm tellin' you now: I'll walk if you try to use me as an excuse for sitting home alone, or to pick a fight with your mother or with Ed. Hey, you do what you gotta do. I ain't judgin'. Just don't blame anybody but yourself if you get my drift. (*Pause*) You get my drift? (*Arnold nods.*) I come down too heavy? (*Shakes his head*) Still want me to stay? (*Arnold nods.*) All right. Now we're dancin'.

ARNOLD: I ever tell you, I think you're swell?

DAVID (*Standing*):   Break this up. I got school tomorrow.

ARNOLD (*Standing*):   You go on ahead. I need an airing.

DAVID: Want company?

ARNOLD: Go on. I'll be up.

DAVID: Okay. See you later.

ARNOLD: David? You're not, are you?

DAVID: What?

ARNOLD (*Embarrassed*):   Straight?

DAVID: What would you do if I was?

ARNOLD: Kill you.

DAVID (*Laughs*):   Nice to know you care. (*Starts to leave*)

ARNOLD: Watch how you cross the street.
            (*The lights fade down and out.*)

SCENE FOUR

Several hours later. The apartment. The lights are out, the couch un-folded, and Ed is asleep in it. Arnold enters in a robe from the bathroom, heading toward the kitchen, weaving, with an empty glass in his hand.

ED (*Waking*):   Huh? What?

ARNOLD: It's me. Go to sleep.

ED: Arnold? Oh. (*Trying to wake*) What time is it?

ARNOLD: Almost six. Go to sleep.

ED: I waited up for you.

ARNOLD: I see.

ED: You want to talk?

ARNOLD: No. Go to sleep.

ED: I don't want to go to sleep.

ARNOLD: So don't go to sleep.

ED: You just get home?

ARNOLD: Awhile ago.

ED: I didn't hear you. Where'd you go? (*No response*) She said she's leaving.

ARNOLD: I know. I tripped over her bags on my way in.

ED: She didn't want to stay the night, but she couldn't get a flight out until morning. When I came in she was walking out to spend the night in the airport. I got her calmed down a little. (*Pause*) She'd stay if you asked her.

ARNOLD: Go to sleep.

ED: Stop telling me to go to sleep.

ARNOLD: All right, go to hell! (*Sorry*) Want a drink?

ED: Sure, white wine. (*Arnold shoots a look.*) Juice. (*As Arnold makes the drinks*) You know, I saw Laurel today. That's where I went. I don't think she's overjoyed with the separation. She told me she's pregnant. She's not, but she said she was to see if I'd go back to her . . . if she was. God. The things that ran through my mind. Baby carriages, walks in the park, my folks playin' with it . . . Quite a sensation. I guess I would've gone back if she was. But then . . . I don't know.

ARNOLD: I hope you didn't tell her that.

ED: Of course I did. After five years of marriage, I'm not going to start lying to her now.

ARNOLD (*Numb*):   What'd she say?

ED: She said she could be . . . if I came back. (*Pause*) She thinks we're sleeping together. Funny, huh? Laurel and your mother thinking the same thing. Maybe they know something we don't. (*Clears his throat*) I suppose it's her way of expressing anger. Laurel. Not your mother. Though I have seen happier women than her. Your mother, that is. (*Arnold is now sitting on the bed. He snickers.*) What's so funny?

ARNOLD: Seems like every time I turn around, here we are: Arnold and Ed in bed together.

ED: Talking.

ARNOLD: Talking. Me with a lump in my throat and you with a foot in your mouth.

ED: Why? What'd I say?

ARNOLD: Don't ask me. I stopped listening years ago.

ED: I don't see what I said that's . . .

ARNOLD: It was nothing. Pay me no mind; I'm drunk.

ED: Look, I know I'm not the most sensitive person in the world . . .

ARNOLD: Ed, take a note: Never fish for compliments in polluted waters.

ED: Are you really drunk?

ARNOLD: I hold it well, don't I? A trick I learned in finishing school. It's done with mirrors. You think I'm here in bed next to you but actually I'm asleep under a table in a bar on Forty-third.

ED (*Amused*): This is the first time I've ever seen you drunk.

ARNOLD: Well, get a good look, Leon, 'cause I'm dryin' out in the morning.

ED: Arnold Beckoff drunk.

ARNOLD: Blottoed, plastered, and plotzed . . . incorporated.

ED: Why'd you get drunk?

ARNOLD (*Knocking on Ed's head*): Hello? Anybody home? Sometimes you really frighten me.

ED (*Offering his arms and shoulder*): Care to talk about it?

ARNOLD: Sure. Why should the neighbors have all the fun? (*Lies back*) I had a genuinely superior motive for drinking this much. Don't tell nobody, but I'm a pushover when I'm drunk. And I thought that if I got good and looped I'd repent and ask my mother to stay. It worked too. Until I got a peek at her sitting in there on the bed with her "Holier-Than-Thou" attitude and her "Merry Martyr" smile. The way she acts you'd think she and God went to school together. She thinks I hate her. I know the way her mind works and she thinks I hate her.

ED: I'm sure she knows you don't.

ARNOLD: Oh, no, she does. She thinks I hate her and everything she stands for. And I don't, for the life of me, know how to tell her that what I want more than anything is to have exactly the life she had. With a few minor alterations. My par-

ents . . . They were something together. In all the years they were married the only time they were separated was for two days while my mother was in the hospital. And my father . . . He wouldn't even get into bed without her. He spent both nights on a chair in the living room. And the way they made my brother and me feel; like we were the smartest, handsomest, most talented, most important two people in the world. Didn't matter what we did, good or bad, it was the best. And she thinks she did something wrong.

ED: Are you really a pushover when you're drunk?

ARNOLD: Earth to Ed. Earth to Ed. Come in, please. (*Ed giggles.*) You've got your own problems don'tcha? C'mon, spill your guts.

ED: David said you haven't gone out since Alan died.

ARNOLD: We're talking about you now.

ED: I can understand you not wanting to at first, but still. You could at least go out for a few drinks, take a quick trip to the backroom. No harm in that.

ARNOLD: You may not understand this, but I want more out of life than meeting a pretty face and sitting down on it. That answer your question?

ED: Graphically.

ARNOLD: I do my best.

ED: If I made a pass at you now . . . Would you let me?

ARNOLD: All right, who spiked the orange juice?

ED: Actually, it's David's idea. He thinks you're pushing chastity too far. He says it's unhealthy.

ARNOLD: This is the first time I've been seduced in the guise of preventive medicine.

ED: I told him I'd consider it.

ARNOLD: What a friend.

ED: I didn't mean it that way.

ARNOLD: You never do.

ED: I mean, this is not exactly what Iwant.

ARNOLD: I came to the same conclusion myself. I think it was the wedding that gave you away.

ED: I didn't want that either. I mean, I did, but it turned out not to be what I want. In fact, it made me less sure than ever about what it is I do want.

ARNOLD: No problem. I've got a Sears catalog you can flip through. If you see it there give a primal scream and I'll get it for your birthday.

ED: You're not being fair.

ARNOLD: I'm upset, uptight, and up to my nipples in Southern Comfort. I'm sorry.

ED: Never mind.

ARNOLD: I said I'm sorry. You're trying to say something and I've got diarrhea of the mouth. Come on, I'll behave. I promise. (*No response*) Hey, this is Arnold here. You can tell me anything.

ED: I want another chance with you.

ARNOLD: Anything but that.

ED: Wait. Just think about it for a minute. It makes a lot of sense. We know each other so well, there'd be no surprises. We know what to expect from each other. You said yourself we have no secrets.

ARNOLD: What'd that kid of mine say to you?

ED: Just listen for a second. Laurel and I together . . . it wasn't enough. Obviously or I wouldn't be here. And that's the point:

I am here. No matter what I do, I always end up back here, with you, in bed . . .

ARNOLD: Talking!

ED: Talking. But here. Arnold, the time I've spent here with you and David . . . it's been the closest thing to whatever it is I want. I feel wonderful here. . . .

ARNOLD: "Don't care if the kid ain't mine, I wanna be the father of your baby." I saw that movie. I even read the book.

ED: Are you finished?

ARNOLD: Ed, please.

ED: Not five minutes ago it's what you said you wanted.

ARNOLD: I thought you weren't listening.

ED: I know you're upset about your mother.

ARNOLD: That's not it. . . .

ED: Okay, so maybe it's too soon after Alan . . .

ARNOLD: Oh, Puh-lease!

ED: I'm asking you to think about it. That's all. Just think.

ARNOLD: Don't you know that I have? How thick can you possibly be? Can't you see that since you called that's all I've thought about? Five days ago you walked through the door and from that moment I've been playing the dutiful wife and mother to your understanding if distant father. And David? He's been having the time of his life playing baby.

ED: And it's been wonderful.

ARNOLD: It's been preposterous. It's a joke. Three grown men playing house!

ED: You think this is playing house? You have no idea what playing house is. Arnold, I love Laurel. That may sound a little strange considering the circumstances, but my feelings for her are genuine and just as strong now as when we got

married. It has, however, become apparent that what we have
is a friendship, not a marriage.

ARNOLD: That's a hell of a lot more than most people have.

ED: I'm almost forty, Arnold. Can you understand what that
means? It means it's time for me to stop jerkin' around. I want
more than a marriage which is at best purposeless, unfulfilling,
but perfectly acceptable. Now, whatever you think of us, you
could never describe us like that.

ARNOLD: Not the perfect part anyway.

ED: Are you through making cracks?

ARNOLD: I just don't see what you think is here that you can't
have with Laurel.

ED: To tell you the truth I'm not sure either. But there's something that's kept me coming back. . . .

ARNOLD: Are you forgetting why we broke up in the first place?
You really think you could bring your friends here? You ready
to introduce me to your parents as your lover and David as
our son? Ed. Angel, I just threw my mother—my *mother*—out
of my house and all she wanted was to not talk about it. You
think I'll ask less from you?

ED: I think it's time to find out.

ARNOLD: I don't know, Ed. Christ, I mean, I don't even know
what this is supposed to be. I can't exactly buy a book or study
some *Reader's Digest* article that's gonna tell me. All I know is
whatever this is, it's not a Grade-B imitation of a heterosexual
marriage. See, I thought that Alan and David and I could find
out together . . . so now . . .

ED: Let me help you find out. You, me, and David.

ARNOLD: I can't.

ED: Why? You scared I'll walk out again? Of course I can't
guarantee anything . . .

ARNOLD: That's not it.

ED: Then is it David? You afraid I'll hurt him?

ARNOLD: I know how you feel about him, I know you wouldn't.

ED: Then what, Arnold?

ARNOLD (*Deep breath*): I am not Laurel.

ED: I'm counting on that.

ARNOLD: Go home, Ed.

ED: Are you crying?

ARNOLD: Leave me alone.

ED: I can't. Not with you like this. You need someone to talk to.

ARNOLD (*Striking out*): I don't need anyone. Thank you.

ED: Well, maybe I do.

ARNOLD: Then go home. You've got a lovely wife who'd do anything for you. She can give you a home, a two-car garage, a child of your own, white picket fence . . . the whole shebang, double-dipped in chocolate and government-approved. Go home, Ed. I ain't got nothin' like that here.

ED: You really believe that? (*Arnold nods.*) Your mother did quite a job on you. (*Teasing*) Hello? Anybody home? You're gonna make me say it, aren't you? Undemonstrative soul that I am, you're gonna make me say it.

ARNOLD: I don't want you to say anything.

ED: Oh no, I'll say it. I'm not ashamed, embarrassed maybe, but not ashamed. But I'll be damned if I say it to your back. (*Pulls Arnold over and pins him down*)

ARNOLD: Ed! For Chrissake!

ED: You ready? Now, you better listen good 'cause I don't know when I'll get the guts to say it again.

ARNOLD: Ed, you're gonna wake my mother.

ED: So, let her hear. I hope they're both listening. Might as well let everyone know. Is everybody listening? Okay. Here goes. Arnold Beckoff . . . I love . . .

DAVID (*Interrupting as he enters*):   What the hell's going on in here?

ED: Perfect timing.

DAVID (*Throwing on the lights: We can now see his black-and-blue eye.*):   Oh, am I interrupting something? I hope, I hope, I hope.

ARNOLD (*Straightening up his appearance*):   You're not, you're not. What're you doing up at this hour?

DAVID: My alarm went off ten minutes ago. In case you love-birds haven't noticed, it's morning.

ED: Jesus!

DAVID: Is this a closed marriage or can anybody join in?

ARNOLD (*As David climbs into bed between them*):   And baby makes three.

ED: My first pajama party.

DAVID (*To Arnold*):   You look awful. Didn't you sleep?

ARNOLD: Nary a wink, blink, or nod.

ED: . . . incorporated.

ARNOLD: Thank you.

ED: Don't mention it.

ARNOLD: Any news from the other camp?

DAVID: I heard shuffling. I think she's ready to leave.

ARNOLD: I'd better splash my face and get ready for the grand exit.

ED (*As Arnold struggles to rise*):   Need help?

ARNOLD: I think my battery's dead. Gimme a boost. (*They shove from behind, Arnold flies to his feet. Then, à la Mae West*) Thanks, boys. (*Exits into bathroom*)

DAVID (*Anxiously*):   Well?

ED: I struck out. He said no.

DAVID: You asked first? Don't you know anything? It don't mean nothin', anyway. Arnold always says no when you ask him a question. Then he thinks about it and . . . Watch. (*Calling out*) Hey, Arnold? You want breakfast?

ARNOLD (*Off*):   No, thanks.

DAVID (*Counts to ten on his fingers*):   Now . . .

ARNOLD (*Off*):   David? Maybe I'll have an egg.

DAVID: Most contrary person I've ever met.

ED (*Getting out of bed*):   We better get dressed. They should be alone for the final round.

DAVID: I am dressed.

ED: Show-off. Well, start the coffee while I catch up. (*Exits*)

DAVID (*Heading to the kitchen*):   Do you like pancakes?

ED (*Off*):   I love pancakes.

DAVID: Great. I'll make you some . . . when I learn to cook. (*He turns on the radio.*)

RADIO: Plaza 6-6654 with your requests. It's six fifty-four in the Big Apple on what looks to be a beautiful June day. And I'm here, with you, dedicated to the one you love. Now an oldie by request, from Beulah to Robert and Michael. Guess she just can't make up her mind. Ha-ha. All right, Beulah, here it is with love. (*Music begins.*) Our number's Plaza 6-6654 and I'm waiting to play one for you. (*Music continues into the scene.*)

ARNOLD (*Entering*):   What're you listening to?

DAVID: One of those call-in shows, I think. Want me to change it?

ARNOLD: No, leave it. I ever tell you about the time Alan phoned in a request to one of those shows? They read the dedication wrong. He announced, "From Ellen to Arnold." He musta thought it was a typo or somethin'.

DAVID: What song was it?

ARNOLD: "My Funny Valentine." (*David retches.*) It was very romantic.

DAVID: Is your mother staying for breakfast?

ARNOLD: Ask her, not me. Has she shown her face yet?

DAVID: Nope.

ARNOLD: Go on in and see if she needs any help.

DAVID (*Dramatically*):   "Into the jaws of death, into the mouth of hell!" Any message?

ARNOLD: No. (*David exits. Arnold folds the couch. Ma screams offstage.*) Not again.

MA (*Enters with David*):   Arnold, did you see this eye? How could you let him walk around with a face like this? (*Drags him to the kitchen*) Come over here. I'm going to put some ice on it.

DAVID: Mrs. Beckoff, it's all right.

MA: All right? You look like an ad for "I'd rather fight than switch."

ARNOLD (*To David's rescue as Ed enters*):   Ma, leave him alone. Ice won't help. He's had it for two days.

MA: What're you talking? I saw him yesterday . . .

ARNOLD: He covered it with makeup so he'd look nice for you.

DAVID: I'm okay. Really. But thanks, anyway.

ED: C'mon, Champ. I'll buy you breakfast out.

DAVID (*Surveying the scene*):   Great. But I gotta do somethin' first. (*Toward bedroom*) I'll be out in a minute.

ED (*Putting on his jacket*):   I guess I'll see you later. (*To Ma*) It was a pleasure meeting you, Mrs. Beckoff.

MA: The pleasure was mine, Ed. I hope you and your wife come to your senses. Couples must learn to live with conflict. After all, a problem is never as permanent as a solution.

ED: Uh . . . thank you. (*Shouting*) David? Hurry up.

ARNOLD: Aren't you going to wash up first?

ED: That's all right. I'm all right. (*Pause. Desperate.*) David!!!

DAVID (*Off*):   I'm comin', already!

ARNOLD (*Taking Ed aside*):   Ed? What we were talking about before? Y'know, six years is a long time . . . I don't know. But we can talk.

ED: That's all I'm asking. (*Trying to control himself*) Good. Good.

DAVID (*Enters with a big grin*):   Here I is.

MA: You take care of that eye.

DAVID: I will. It was nice meeting you. (*To Ed*) Remember your wallet this time? (*Ed checks.*) See you later, Arnold. (*Gives him a peck on the cheek*)

ARNOLD: Have a nice day. And don't come home before school's over!

DAVID (*To Ed*):   You look like someone kicked you in the head. (*They exit. David sticks his head back in.*) And you two play like nice children. (*Out*)

ED (*Off*):   Yahoo!

ARNOLD (*Holding back a laugh*):   He likes the wallpaper. Covers a multitude of sins.

MA (*Bringing her bags to the door*):   I'll be leaving myself, now.

ARNOLD: You don't have to fly back to Florida. You could stay . . .

MA: With your brother? No. It's better if he doesn't know about this. I'll call him from Miami, tell him I changed my plans and couldn't make it up this week.

ARNOLD: I'm going to tell him what happened.

MA (*Angry*): Do what you want. I don't care.

ARNOLD: Ma, it's important that he knows. He's part of this family too.

MA: What else do you want to do to me? What, Arnold, what? You want me to leave? I'm leaving. You want me to fight? I'm too tired. You want me to change? I'm too old and I can't. I can't, I can't, I can't. So you do what you have to do, and I'll do what I have to do and I hope you're satisfied. (*Arnold groans.*) If I had ever opened a mouth to my mother like you did to me, you'd be talking to a woman with a size six Wedgie sticking out of her forehead. But I didn't raise my children like that. I wanted them to respect me because they wanted to. Not because I beat it in to them. Go know.

ARNOLD: Do we have to start this again?

MA: Yes. Because you can't put all the blame on me. It's not fair. Some of it was my fault, but not all. You think I didn't know about you, Arnold? Believe me, I knew. And not because you told me. I didn't need you to tell me. I knew but I said no. I hoped . . . What's the difference, I knew and I turned my back. But I wasn't the only one. There are other things you should have told me. You opened a mouth to me about your friend Alan. . . . How was I supposed to know?

ARNOLD: Why? You would have understood?

MA: Maybe. Maybe not. You can't know for sure. But I flew up for the funeral and you never said a word.

ARNOLD: So you could've done what? Tell me he's better off dead?

MA: Or maybe I could've comforted you. Told you what to expect. You and your "widowing." (*She turns to leave, stops, takes a breath. One last try.*) And about this Ed: You love him?

ARNOLD: I don't know. I think so.

MA: Like you loved Alan?

ARNOLD: No. They're very different. Alan loved all my faults: my temper, my bitchiness, my fat. . . . He looked for faults to love. And Ed? Ed loves the rest. And really, who needs to be loved for their virtues? Anyway, it's easier to love someone who's dead; they make so few mistakes.

MA: You've got an unusual way of looking at things, Arnold Beckoff.

ARNOLD: Runs in the family. Ma, I miss him so much.

MA: Give yourself time, Arnold. It gets better. But, Arnold, it won't ever go away. You can work longer hours, adopt a son, fight with me . . . whatever, it'll still be there. But that's all right. It becomes part of you, like wearing a ring or a pair of glasses. You get used to it and it's good . . . because it makes sure you don't forget. You don't want to forget him, do you? (*Arnold shakes his head.*) So, it's good. (*Pause*) I guess that's what I would have said . . . (*The phone rings*) if I'd known. You'd better answer that. It may be something with that . . . son of yours.

(*Arnold goes to the phone. As soon as he's turned his back, Ma slips out the door with her bags. Arnold doesn't notice.*)

ARNOLD (*Answering*): Hello. . . . Hi, Murray. . . . What? . . . The radio? It's on. . . . All right, hang on. (*He puts the phone down and goes to the radio, turning up the volume.*) It's Murray, something about the radio.

RADIO (*Mid-sentence*): . . . no, I've just checked with my producer, who took the call, and he's confirmed it. What a morning. Whatever is this world coming to? So, here it is, a dedication from David to Arnold with all his love . . .

(*Music begins to play. It is Big Maybelle singing "I Will Never Turn My Back on You."*)

ARNOLD: How do you like that? That's some kid I got there, huh? (*Turning*) You hear that, Ma? (*Sees she's gone*) Ma? (*Goes to door*) Ma?

Runs to window and looks out as the music plays. He turns toward the audience and listens to the song calmly. As the music ends, the lights fade and the curtain falls.

THE END

HARVEY FIERSTEIN is a recipient of a Rockefeller Foundation Grant in Playwrighting, a Ford Foundation Grant for new American Plays, a CAPS fellowship, a special OBIE Award for writing and acting, four *Villager* Awards, the *Soho News* Commendation for Best New American Play, a Corporation for Public Broadcasting grant, the Fund for Human Dignity Award, two Drama Desk nominations, the George Oppenheimer/*Newsday* Playwrighting Award, an Association of Comedy Artists Award, and the Hull/Warriner Award from the Dramatists Guild. He is also the winner of the 1983 Tony Award for Best Actor and Best Play for *Torch Song Trilogy*. This marks the first time in Tony history that one person has won awards in these two categories for the same play.

With a Fine Arts degree from Pratt Institute, Mr. Fierstein began his writing career in 1973. Beyond his current Broadway presentation, *Torch Song Trilogy*, he has two new works slated for production this coming season: *Spookhouse*, a full-length play for Off Broadway, and a musical comedy, *La Cage aux Folles*, with music and lyrics by Jerry Herman, to be directed by Arthur Laurents. Mr. Fierstein is also now writing an original teleplay for P.B.S., entitled *Kaddish and Old Men*.

Born June 6, 1954, in Brooklyn, Harvey began his acting career as a founding member of The Gallery Players, a Brooklyn-based community theater group that is still in existence. He made his professional acting debut with Andy Warhol in 1971 at La Mama E.T.C. With more than 60 productions to his credit, Harvey has also appeared in numerous films, most recently as the voice of the Devil in the television film *The Demon Murder Case.*

As owner of two dogs (Georges and Bubbie) and a rabbit (Arnold), Harvey's interests are varied. In his spare time between writing and acting he collapses.